INTERIOR DESIGN

インテリア デザイン

発想と設計 小森谷 賢二

by KENJI KOMORIYA

CONTENTS

目次

はじめに

本書は、私がアトリエ・ヴィンチを主宰してから今日までの14年間の仕事の中から24物件といくつかのプロダクトを選び、その発想から設計のプロセスまでを解説したものである。

当然のことながら、物件ごとに立地条件やクライアントからの要望も異なり、その解法についても、そのたびにそれぞれの物件に合った方法を考え、プレゼンテーションや設計プロセスも様々である。ここでは作品の写真だけでなく、エスキスや模型写真、図面等もつけているので、そのことが良くお分かりいただけることと思う。設計事務所によって色々な方法があるが、そのひとつとして見ていただきたい。

CGやCADによる作図化が進む中で、自らの手でスケッチを描き、模型をつくり、現場に足を運び、空間のリアリティを確かめながら設計をしていくことの重要性も、伝えたかったことのひとつである。

自分の仕事を一度整理する目的で企画したものであるが、読者にとって何らかの参考になれば幸いである。

Introduction

This book presents the envisioning and planning processes behind 24 buildings and several products which I have worked on in the fourteen years since I opened studio Vinci.

Needless to say, for every structure there is a unique set of construction circumstances and client wishes, all calling for various solutions, and all requiring different presentation and planning approaches. Here I have presented not only photos of finished buildings, but also plans, photos of models and various drawings to enable the reader to grasp these processes. Planning offices have various methods of operating; this book should be viewed as one such approach.

Even in the midst of the CG and CAD revolution it is important to me to make hand sketches and models, and to visit the building site, in order to know the spatial requirements of the location, and I have wished to stress this point in the following pages. While I originally planned this book as a means of putting my own work in order, I hope readers will find it to be a useful reference.

インテリアデザインについて

私の設計の手法

私の設計の手法は、幾何学的な形を組み合わせるとか、グリッドによるレイアウトといったものではない。まず現場に立ち、その場を感じ、感じたそこにあるエネルギーを形にしていくのである。

その場のエネルギーとは、行き交う人々の動きからくるものであり、飛び交う情報や新しい創造力であったり、堆積した歴史、人々の記憶、時には人々の欲望であったりする。

こんなエネルギーはもちろん、与えられた物理的空間内におとなしく収まっているわけではない。多分に流動的なもので、たえず増大したり、収縮したりする。私はこんなエネルギーを追いかけるようにデザインをしていく。すると、流れるような線が生まれ、固まりができ、よどんだ溜まりの「間」が生まれ、すき間もでき、デザインが外へ飛び出すこともある。

ほとんどの設計者が、与えられた敷地や空間の中でいかに必要な機能を整然と美しく納めようかと考える。そのため、よくまとまってはいるが、こじんまりとしたデザインに終わってしまう。私の場合は、そのような物理的条件から設計を発想しないため、その空間から解放された自由さをもち、デザインもその場にふさわしいエネルギーをもつことになる。

光について

デザインはクライアントの要望を満たすべく機能的であることは当然であるが、単に斬新であったり、美しいだけでは目的を達したことにならない。人を幸せな気持ちにしたり、優しい気持ちにしたり、安心感を与えたり、時にはドキドキさせたり、こんな人々の感情を操作する、そのことこそ、人との距離が近く、触れられ、使われるインテリアデザインの重要な目的である。

人々が過ごす、滞留するインテリア空間には、通過するための空間であっても、時間が介在する。そのため、目に見える部分だけのデザインではなく、時間の経過とともに感じる空間をデザインしなければならない。

デザインの構成要素の中で光はとりわけ重要なものである。色も形も光を与えなければ、その存在すら目にすることはできないのだ。そして光は人の心の奥深い部分を操作するものである。レストランでキャンドルをはさみ、カップルは恋を語らい、暖炉の火を囲み、家族は安らぎを得る。温かさだけでなく、光は空間に中心をうみだすのである。照明は火や太陽の光の役割を人工的につくり出すものであるが、永い間にその意味は忘れられ、不必要に明るいだけの空間があふれるようになった。人々の感情に訴える空間をつくるには、光を効果的に制御し、その本来の意味を思い出し、巧みに利用しなければならない。

素材について

私は素材の中では特にスティールとガラスが好きだ。木や大理石といった有機的な素材は、デザインする上ではあまり好まない。

それらは、デザインする以前に、すでに永い時間と自然の力による存在感と意味をもっているからである。私は、素材そのものがあまり意味をもたない無機質なものが好きだ。それらはすべてただの材料である。形を与えられ、それぞれが互いに関係をもってトータルな空間を構成した時、初めてデザインという意味をもつのである。

しかし私も全く木や大理石を使わないわけで

On Interior Design

My Planning Method

My method of planning does not use combinations of geometric forms or a grid-based layout. Instead, it involves visiting a building site, getting a feel for a place, and giving shape to the energy felt there.

When I speak of the energy of a place, I mean the energy that comes from people who work and interact there, the interplay of information and new creative forces, the history of the place, the memories and even the desires of the people associated with it. This kind of energy is of course not something that neatly fills a physical space. Rather, it is probably fluid, expanding and contracting all the time. But it is this energy that I pursue in my design work. In so doing flowing lines are created, shapes solidify, a settled "space" is born, openings emerge; in short, a design springs forth.

When considering the landscape and space of a building site most architects will attempt to meet the requirements of the facility in a natural and aesthetically pleasing way. Designs produced in this way are usually orderly but often cramped. With my approach the design does not originate from such physical considerations, but maintains its freedom from spatial limitations, and possesses an energy appropriate to that place.

On Light

A design must offer the functionality to satisfy the demands of the client, but it is not enough simply to devise a fresh and beautiful design.

A design must give people a happy feeling, or a gentle feeling, or a feeling of safety, even, at times, a sense of excitement. An interior design must manipulate the person's sentiments, moving them closer, touching them, encouraging them to use the space.

People spend time in an interior, and then are absent from it. A space is both a place which is occupied and a place where time intercedes. For this reason, one cannot design a space for the eyes only; one must also create a space which gives a sense of the passage of time.

For this reason light is a very important element of the design structure. In order for shape and color to exist they must be given light. Light affects people deeply. A couple will talk of love at a candlelit table in a restaurant, or a family will rest around a fireplace in the home. Light not only warms a place, but gives birth to a spatial center. Originally, illumination was created to simulate the light of the sun and fire, but over time this purpose has been forgotten, and more and more space has been illuminated unnecessarily. To create a space the gives feeling to people one must use lighting effectively, recollecting its original purpose, and using it as skillfully as possible.

On Materials

Of all materials I prefer in particular steel and glass. Organic materials such as wood and granite do not fit with my style of design. I feel that such materials are invested with a significance and presence derived from the power of nature and history even before I use them. I prefer to work with inorganic materials which have no particular meaning. They are nothing more or less than materials. By giving them shape, and relationships within the structure of a total space, they take on the meaning of design for the first time.

However, this is not to say that I never use

はない。住宅やレストランといった空間では安心感が最も重要な要素であり、人の触れる部分には、緊張感をうむガラスや冷たいスティールなどは決して使わず、日常的な木を用いている。

インテリアデザイナーの役割

私のデザインにおけるキーワードをいくつかあげると"都会性""現代性""未来""スピード"である。このように並べるとずいぶんと偏っているように思われるかもしれない。しかしデザインとは、現在を分析し、未来のありようを考え、常に進化していかねばならないものである。また、とりわけ変化が激しく、デザインを必要としているのが都会である。古いものにも良いデザインがあり、新しいものばかり追求することだけがデザインではない、と言う人がいる。確かに、過去のものにも素晴らしいデザインがあるのは事実である。いや、人間の身体は機能や生理については昔から何も変わっておらず、デザインについても追求し尽くされ、我々を充分に満足させるものが全て出揃っているとも言える。また、様々な国や地域でも生活に必要なもの

が、それぞれの風土や文化に根ざして理想的な形となり、伝承されているのである。しかし、すでに認知されている過去のデザインを部分的に変えて使ったり、組み合わせで新しく見せようとするのはコーディネートであり、デザインではない。

私が言いたいのは、コーディネート自体を否定しようということではない。むしろ人々が求めているのは、リゾート風の空間であったり、ヨーロッパ風のクラシックな空間であったりする。私自身、スペイン風タイルと白塗りの家が好きである。しかしデザイナーとして仕事をする時、常に将来に向けて新たな可能性を探り、それを形に変えて提案していくのがその役割だと考えている。

都市との関わり

インテリアデザインが都市より隔離され、閉じ込められた内部空間だと思っている人が多い。いや実際、都市との関わりを考えず、無責任にモノ（あえてこのようなモノをデザインとは呼ばない）をつくっている設計者がほとんどである。しかし、プライベートな住宅の内装を除き、店舗は通りに対してファサー

ドをもち、オフィスビルもガラス張りの部分を介して内部空間は通りに対して開かれている。歩行者のアイレベルにおいて、ショッピングストリートではこのような店舗の連続が都市の表情であり、オフィスビル街でもやはり一階のインテリアの連続が都市の顔をつくっているのである。

資本主義のもとで、他店よりも売上げを伸ばさなければいけない競争原理の上で、我々はクライアントから仕事をもらっているわけだが、差別化だけで都市に対して無責任にモノをつくっていくと、通りや都市は雑然として醜くなり、結局人々からいずれ見捨てられてしまうであろう。

ファッションにおいて、ひとつひとつのアイテムが有名なブランドであっても、コーディネートによっては下品なスタイルになってしまうことがある。都市も同じである。それぞれの空間が個性的で美しいものでありながら、同時に通りや都市とのハーモニーがあるように、個々のデザイナーが自覚しなければならない。それは都市計画や法的規制を語る以前にあるべき、意識の問題なのである。

wood or granite. In homes and restaurants a sense of security is of the utmost importance. Hence, in places where human contact and touch is most likely, I never use steel or glass, opting instead for the usual types of wood.

The Role of Interior Designers

Some of my keywords are "urban," "modern," "future" and "speed." Bunched together like this these terms probably create the impression of a very slanted viewpoint. However, design must remain in a state of evolution, observing the present and predicting the patterns of the future. Moreover, the radical changes which are ongoing in the cities create the need for design. On the other hand, there are excellent old designs, and some people claim that simply creating new designs is not in fact true design at all. And it is certainly true that the past is full of fine designs. After all,the functions and physical nature of humans has not changed since ancient times, and virtually everything necessary to satisfy our needs has been produced in the designs of the past. The unique living requirements of the diverse lands and environments of the world

have all been met with ideal, traditional solutions that have been passed down to the present! .

However, simply taking apart these traditional forms and putting them back together again in new shapes is not design, but coordinating. And I do not wish to say that I deny the value of coordinating. Rather, people want a resort style space, or a classic European style space. Personally, I like the red tile and white-washed walls of Spanish architecture. However, when I work as a designer, I look to the future and search for new possibilities. It is the role of the designer to propose forms for those ideas.

Relating to the City

There are many people who believe the purpose of interior design is to enclose a space, in order to separate that space from the urban environment. In fact, most designers take this irresponsible approach to creating things (we should not call these things "designs," either.) However, with the exception of home interiors, stores have facades that open on to streets, and office buildings also show their interiors to the streets through glass fronts. For pedestrians, this

continuous line-up of shopfronts forms the expression of the city, and the same is true of first floor offices, which likewise form the eye-level "face" of the city.

Under capitalism each store must compete with others to increase its sales, and that is the reason we receive work. But in the effort to create conspicuous presences the cities themselves are treated irresponsibly. Streets and urban areas grow increasingly disorderly, and the result is that people finally abandon them.

In the world of fashion merchandising certain brand items can become very famous, but thrown together in an uncoordinated way their effect is vulgar. The city is no different. Even while individual spaces might have their own particular appeal, every designer must take into consideration how they harmonize with the streets and cities in which they are located. And this is the duty of the designer regardless of city ordinances or legislative guidelines.

JINGUMAE MEDIA SQUARE
神宮前メディア・スクエア
SHIBUYA − TOKYO
東京−渋谷

東京、渋谷の明治通り沿いに建つビルである。1階にテレビスタジオ、地下の駐車場をはさんで、地下2階にこのスタジオの受付、ロビー、事務所、役者控室、メイク室、リハーサル室、編集室等がある。3～8階はテナントフロアで、9階が再びスタジオホールとなっている。

エントランスホールは、床の御影石のパターンを前庭まで連続させ、ガラススクリーンを通して外部と一体化したパブリックスペースとなるようにした。ホールの天井高は、通常のビルの三層分の高さをもっているが、これに対して奥行きが浅いため、壁が威圧的にならぬようガラススクリーンを施し、内部に照明を仕込み、光壁とした。この巨大な窓、あるいはブラウン管を見る時、ここに壁としての存在は感じられない。

地下2階のロビーでもエントランスホールの手法をくり返し、壁の一面を光壁としている。窓から射し込む外光のような効果は、そこが地下であることを忘れさせてくれる。

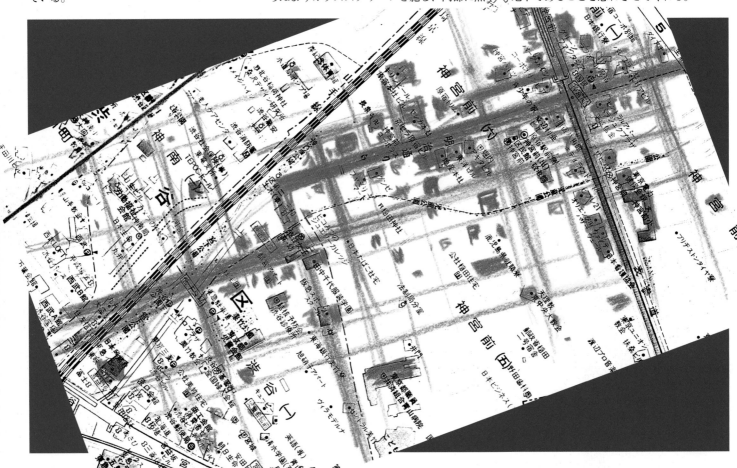

This building stands on Jingumae Street in Shibuya, Tokyo. The first floor is a TV studio, the first basement level a parking garage, and the second basement level the reception desk for the studio, as well as the lobby, the office, the actor's rooms, the make-up rooms, the rehearsal room and the editing offices. Floors three to eight are tenant floors, and the ninth is floor yet another studio hall.

The pattern of the granite floor in the entrance way continues into the front courtyard, which is visible through a glass screen, creating a unified space for this public area. The ceiling of this space is about three times the height of an average building, but the depth of the space is shallow. A glass screen was used to alleviate the sense of confinement, with interior illumination designed to create a wall of light. This huge wall of glass, like a TV screen, is not felt as a barrier.

The same design was used in the lobby of the second basement level as in the entrance, where one of the walls is a "wall of light."

私は建築事務所（アルキメディア設計研究所）から依頼を受けて、このビルの設計段階からプロジェクトに参加した。すでに建築の設計については、ほとんどの部分が決定していたが、インテリアについてはまだ十分に建築的調整をすることができた。
建築のコンセプトを確認した上で設計に入り、プレゼンテーションを行い、再びコンセプト上のずれがないよう話し合い、基本設計を完成させた。私が担当したのは、ビル前面の床、1階のエントランスホールとエレベーターホール、TVスタジオのホワイエである。そして地下2階の全フロア；ここは1階のTVスタジオを運営するための全機能、受付、ロビー、事務所、役者控室、メイク室、リハ

ーサル室、シャワー室、編集室等がある特殊フロアである。
建築工事が着工された後、実施設計に入り、建築設計側の若干の修正、改良と並行して、インテリアについても見直しを行い、基本設計において時間がなく残されていた部分を含め、建築のコンセプトをより明確に表現するデザインへと設計を煮詰めることができた。
これは、この間多くの機会と時間をかけて、建築の設計者である小林正美氏と話し合うことができ、氏の考えを理解し、私自身がこのビルと都市の関わりについて明確な答えをもつことができたからである。
"閉じた建築"では、通りを形づくるただの壁になってしまう。安全で楽しく美しい街をつ

くるために、建築は積極的に都市と関わりをもち、都市に対して開かれていかねばならない。
「パブリックスペースを介して都市に開いた建築」は小林氏のこのビルのコンセプトでもあり、歩道と後退したビルの間のパブリックスペースは、ガラススクリーンを通してエントランスホールへと連続している。
外部の床は、黒緑の御影石とライトグレーの御影石によるパターンを施し、これをそのまま中へと入り込ませることで、エントランスホールのパブリックスペース化をより明確にした。この床パターンは、さらにエレベーターホール、ホワイエへと連続して、これらの空間にも解放感を与えている。

I received the order for this job by Archi-media architects & associates and participated in the project from the planning stage. Most of the planning for the building was already complete at the time, but I was asked to do much of the architectural survey work for the interior.

After agreeing on the architectural concept the planning was begun, a presentation was made, and another meeting held to confirm that there were no disagreements about the concept. Basic planning was then completed. I supervised work on all of the flooring, the elevator and entrance halls on the first floor, and the hallway of the studio. I also handled the entire second basement floor, a special floor which houses all the support for the studio, including the reception desk, the lobby, the office, the actors' rooms, the

make-up rooms, the rehearsal room, the showers and the editing offices.

After construction had begun preparation of the working drawings commenced. Revisions and improvements to the architectural and interior plans were made, and additions to the basic plan completed, with the full expression of all details which had been left out for lack of time, etc. I spent many hours on many separate occasions discussing these matters with Masami Kobayashi, the building architect, and as a result received all the answers necessary to arrive at an understanding of the relationship of this building to the city.

As the term "closed architecture" suggests, this type of design simply creates a wall. In order to build a safe, pleasant and beautiful city, structures must interact positively with the city,

remaining open to it.

"A building open to the city by way of its public space" was Masami Kobayashi's concept in this plan. The building is connected to the pedestrian sidewalk by way of a public space, with a glass screen standing in front of the entrance hall.

The outer floor is a pattern of green-black and white granite blocks. By continuing this same flooring material into the entrance hall the public quality of the entire space is made more evident. This same pattern is also used on the floors of the elevator hall and the hallway, lending these locations an open feeling.

The glass screen of the entrance hall allows a view of the inner walls, which are three stories high, and this view becomes the building's facade

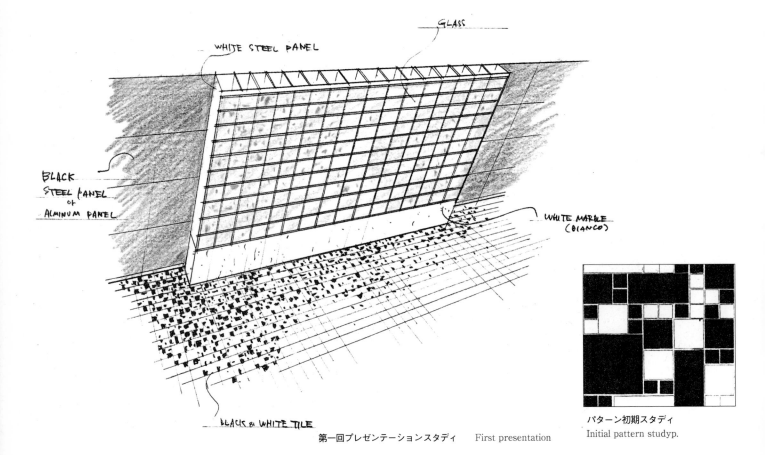

第一回プレゼンテーションスタディ　　First presentation

パターン初期スタディ
Initial pattern studyp.

エントランスホールの壁は、外壁のガラススクリーンを通して外から全て見え、その高さも通常のビルの三層分あるため、歩行者からはここが事実上ビルのファサードとなる。ここを光壁にすることは、今回のインテリアの設計の依頼を受け、建築の説明を受けた時にすぐに思いつき、その後の見直しの中でも迷うことはなかった。このデザインの意図は、まず第一にエントランスホールの高さに比べて奥行きが極端に浅いことから、通常の仕上げや、オブジェを取りつけるといった方法では圧迫感がありすぎるため、ここに壁の概念を超えた別の要素をもってくることで、その存在を消去しようとしたところにある。壁全体に施されたフロストガラスの裏には照明を内蔵し、それは外光の射す巨大な窓ガラスのようになる。重い壁は薄いガラススクリーンとなり、人々はその向こう側にさらに空間を感じるのである。

第二は、外部からはここはレンガの外壁でフレーミングされた形に見え、光壁にすることで、巨大なブラウン管に見立てられ、またそのガラスに施された高密度のパターンからコンピューター回路をもイメージさせ、神宮前メディアスクエアと名づけられたこのビルの目的と存在を外に対して視覚的に伝えることができるからである。原宿と渋谷の中間に位置するこの大きな光のスクリーンは、道行く人々にとって電脳都市にふさわしいランドマークとなることであろう。

to pedestrians viewing it from outside. Having been commissioned to do this interior and hearing an explanation of the architecture I immediately thought of this "wall of light," and never experienced any doubt in its regard. The intention of this design was to alleviate the effect of the very shallow depth of the interior, which would have been overly constrained by the usual solution of placing an object within it. Hence the idea of doing away altogether with the wall. By making the entire front out of frosted glass, with built-in backlighting, it became a single huge window, effectively reflecting away the light from outside. Instead of a massive wall the front is a thin glass screen, through which the observer can experience the space beyond.

Secondly, because the brick wall of the building creates a frame around this "wall of light," it appears much like a huge television screen. The delicate but very detailed pattern etched into the glass resembles a computer circuit, adding visual reinforcement to the purpose and existence of a building which is aptly named "Jingumae Media Square Building." This large screen of light, which stands halfway between Harajuku and Shibuya, is an appropriate landmark to passersbys in this city of the "electronic mind."

製作に先立ってサンプルにより光の効果の実験がおこなわれた

Before manufacturing begins experiments are done with samples to determine the effects of light.

模型による光り壁の検討
Using a model to judge the "wall of light."

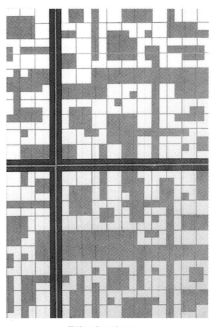

最終の光り壁パターン
Finalized pattern for "wall of light."

上. 左.　外部よりエントランスホールを見る
　　　　床石パターンは外部から内部へと連続している
下.　　　ビル全景
右頁上.　エントランスホール光壁
　　　　フロストガラスにシルクスクリーンにより都市パターンがプリント
　　　　されている
右頁左.　ホワイエ側からエントランスホール、エレベーターホールを見る
右頁右.　ホワイエ。壁は黒のスチールパネルと白大理石が対面している

Upper left: The entrance hall as seen from outside. The pattern of floor stones continues outside.
Bottom: The entire building.
Right page top: The wall of light in the entrance hall.
A silk-screen pattern of the city is printed on the frosted glass.
Right page upper left: The entrance hall and elevator hall as seen from the hallway side.
Right page right side: The hallway
Steel paneling and white granite face each other in the hallway.

都市図がステンレスのエレベータードアにエッチングされている
A diagram of the city is etched into the steel door of the elevator.

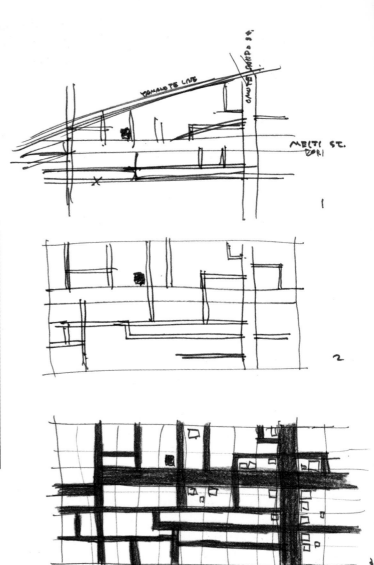

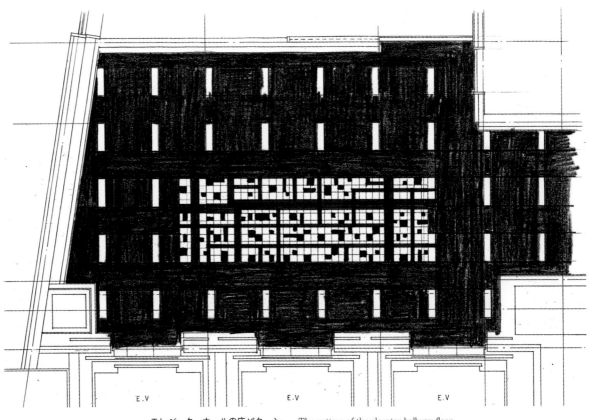

エレベーターホールの床パターン　　The pattern of the elevator hallway floor.

光壁のガラスのパターンは、当初コンピューター回路を連想させるための単なる構成でしかなかった。しかし実施設計に入り、都市と建築のあり方を考えていくうちに、都市の構図そのものをパターンに映し込んでいくことを思いついた。不連続で混沌とした東京の街並みはそのまま複雑な回路、あるいは通信網のようにも見える。そして、このパターンをデザインすることで、抽象的ながら都市に対して何らかのメッセージを込めることができるのではないかと考えた。

パターンは、このビルの周辺状況である原宿から渋谷一帯の都市図をデフォルメ、あるいは整理していきながら、バランスをとって作成した。これをエレベーターホールの床に使い、対面する天井にも簡素化した形で使用している。さらにエレベータードアのエッチングパターンにも応用している。エントランスホールの光壁は、このパターンの一部を取り出して整理し、二つのパターンを作成した。これらをランダムにくり返すことで、高密度に際限なく連続する東京の構図としたのである。

地下2階は、TVスタジオのスタジオ以外の機能をもつ特殊フロアである。ここではエレベーターホールを改めてスタジオのエントランスホールと位置づけた。ダイナミックに湾曲するフロストガラスの光壁と、天井の光のラインでロビーへと導かれるようになっている。

ロビーは天然木で仕上げ、落ちついた雰囲気を出しているが、正面奥の壁は1階エントランスホールの光壁をくり返している。しかしここではパターンではなく、実際のニューヨークの空撮写真をデザイン化し、都市図を具体的な形で見せている。至近距離に光壁があるため、1階と同じパターンでは目が疲れてしまうし、空からの写真で都市を見下ろすことで地下にいることを忘れさせ、さらに外光のような光により、地下の感覚を消去しようとしたものである。ロビーの天井はスケルトンで、部分的に吊り天井とし、スタジオのセットのように見せている。片隅のバーカウンターの天井はアルミの波板で、スタジオという機能中心の固いイメージをやわらげている。通路の天井の一部にもこのアルミの波板を使用している。

地下2階エレベーターホール及びロビーの模型　Layout of the second basement floor hallway and lobby.

Initially the pattern etched onto the glass of the "wall of light" was meant to suggest a computer circuit. However, in light of the relationship of the building to the city, it was later decided to use a schematic of the city for the pattern on the glass. The generally discontinuous and crowded arrangement of the urban sprawl appears in this way like a complex computer circuit or communications network. While symbolic, it was felt that the design of this pattern would also convey a certain kind of message to the city.

The pattern is a deformation and rearrangement of the layout of Harajuku and Shibuya, the districts surrounding the site of the building. This pattern is used on the floor of the elevator hallway, and is also seen in simplified form on the ceiling above. It was likewise applied to the pattern etched into the elevator doors. For the wall of light at the entrance, one part of this pattern was used to create two motifs, which were then repeated randomly many times to suggest the dense and continuous spread of Tokyo.

The second basement floor of the building is a special floor which contains all the facilities of the TV studio with the exception of the studio itself. Here the elevator hall is once again given the rank of an entrance hall, with a dynamically curved frosted glass wall of light and lines of ceiling light which lead the visitor into toward the lobby.

The lobby is made of natural wood, offering a subdued ambience, but the back wall again utilizes the wall of light seen at the entrance. Here, however, the pattern in the glass is not abstract, but is designed from an aerial photograph of New York City, showing a concrete realization of the city. Rather than tire the eyes with a repetition of the pattern seen on the entrance hall glass, this view from above over a cityscape mitigates the sense of being underground, as does the light radiating from the glass. The ceiling of the lobby is skeletal, or hanging in places, suggesting a studio set. The ceiling over the bar counter in the corner is waved aluminum, easing the rigid sense of being in a highly functional studio. The same waved aluminum is also used in the hallway.

1. エレベーターホール　Elevator hall
2. 受付　Reception desk
3. ロビー　Lobby
4. バーカウンター　Counter bar
5. 事務所　Office
6. メイクアップ室　Make-up rooms
7. リハーサル室　The rehearsal room
8. 男子トイレ　The men's restroom
9. 女子トイレ　The women's restroom
10. 役者控室　The actors' rooms
11. 編集室　The editing rooms
12. CGルーム　The CG rooms

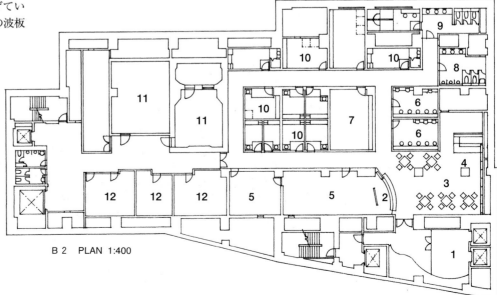

B 2　PLAN 1:400

エレベーターホールの天井照明ルーバーには、対面する床パターンをくり返し、中心性を出している
ドアのパターンはさらに高密度となり、都市図をより明確にしている

The lighting louvers in the elevator hall repeat the pattern on the floor, creating a centralized effect.
The pattern on the door is even finer, showing a more detailed representation of the city map.

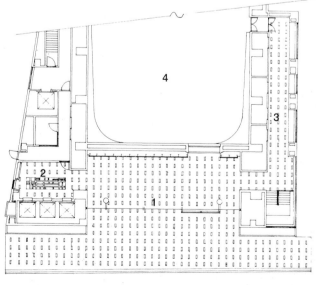

1 st PLAN 1:400

1. エントランスホール　　Entrance hall
2. エレベーターホール　　Elevator hall
3. ホワイエ　　　　　　　Patio
4. ＴＶスタジオ　　　　　TV studio

地下２階エレベーターホール
ガラスドアには電子錠が組み込まれている
光り壁は12mmのフロストガラスの裏に蛍光灯を内蔵している
天井の光の束はロビーへと流れ込み、視覚的な導線となっている

Elevator hall on second basement floor.
The glass door is equipped with an electronic lock.
The 12mm frosted wall glass contains fluorescent back-lighting.
The lighting bundles on the ceiling flow into the lobby, creating a visual guideline.

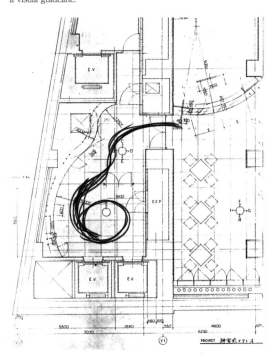

左頁.　　　受付カウンター
上／下左.　受付カウンターよりロビーを見る
　　　　　天井は吊り天井で、ＴＶのセットのように見せている..。壁、天井と
　　　　　もに建築法規により不燃とするために、スチールパネルの下地に不
　　　　　燃処理された天然木シートを貼っている
　　　　　光壁は空撮したニューヨークの写真をコラージュし、ここでは都市
　　　　　図を具体的な形で見せている
下左.　　　バーカウンター
　　　　　天井はアルマイトの波型パネルを曲面で仕上げ、直線的空間にやわ
　　　　　らかさを与えている

Left page: The reception counter
Top and lower left: The lobby as viewed from the reception counter.
The ceiling is a hanging ceiling, suggestive of a TV set Construction regulations
prohibit use of combustible materials in walls and ceilings, hence natural wood
sheeting, treated to be fireproof, was used as backing under the steel paneling.
The frieze on the glass wall-light is a collage created from an aerial photograph of
New York City.
Lower left: The counter bar. The ceiling is made of rounded, waved alumite
sheeting, designed to soften the perpendicular lines of the interior space.

左頁．女性用トイレとシャワー室
上．　　スタッフ用トイレ
右．　　ＣＧルーム前通路
　　　　天井はアルミの波型板
右下．ＣＧルーム前の通路よりロビー方向を見る
左中．男性用トイレ
左下．通路より男性用、女性用トイレを見る

Left page : The women's restroom and shower.
Top : The staff restroom.
Right : The hall in front of the CG rooms.
Waved aluminum sheeting of the ceiling.
Lower right : Looking toward the lobby from the hall
by the CG rooms.
Middle left : The men (IUs restroom.
Lower left : The men's and women's restrooms as
seen from the hall.

NEWS BROADCASTING JAPAN
ニューズ・ブロードキャスティング・ジャパン

SHIBUYA‐TOKYO
東京－渋谷

CS放送を主要業務とする外資系企業のオフィスである。エントランスホールとレセプションホールは、外来の客が訪れる場所で、企業の顔となる空間である。TV放送は、BS、CSへと次々と新しいシステムが導入されている。このように技術発展のめざましいデジタル時代の放送会社にふさわしく、クリーンでハイテックなインテリアデザインとした。
まず、エレベーターホールとレセプションホールはどちらも小さなな空間であるが、一体化させることで大きく感じられるようにした。エレベーターを降りた客は、当社の番組映像を流す４台のモニターTVに迎えられる。そして、曲面加工とフロスト加工を施したハーフミラーガラスの流れるような壁により、レセプションホールへと導かれる。ステンレスを多用した受付カウンターを取り囲むようなガラスの壁の上部には、再び８台のモニ

ーTVにより番組の映像が流されている。
オフィスに入る自動ドアはアルマイト製で、この空間をよりSF映画的な感じにしている。オフィス部分も、会議室と９つの役員室の全てを、パターンを施したフロストガラスで仕切り、レセプションホール同様、クリーンでハイテックなデザインとした。

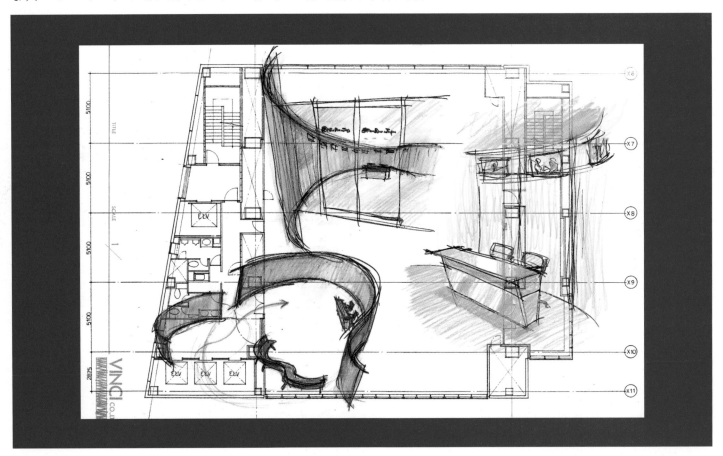

This is the office of a foreign company involved primarily in CS broadcasting. The entrance hall and reception hall are the meeting places for visitors, and thus serve as the "face" of the company. TV broadcasting has evolved from BS to CS as the media continues to develop new systems. A clean, high-tech interior design was required for this digital-age broadcasting company. The entrance and reception halls are both small spaces, but by unifying them they feel

much larger. People exiting the elevators will see the company's broadcast on four TV monitors. The curved, frosted glass wall leads one toward the reception hall. On top of the glass wall, which surrounds the stainless steel reception counter, are another eight TV monitors showing the company's broadcasts. The automatic door that leads into the office is made of aluminum, giving this space an SF movie atmosphere. The locations within the office, including nine directors

offices and a conference room, are separated by the same decorative frosted glass, repeated the clean, high-tech design found in the reception hall.

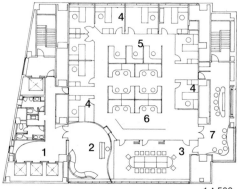

1.	エレベーターホール	Elevator hall
2.	受付ホール	Reception hall
3.	会議室	Conference room
4.	役員室	Directors' offices
5.	秘書ワークステーション	Secretary's work station
6.	一般事務ワークステーション	General office work station
7.	ランチルーム・バー	Lunch room & bar

1：500

レセプションホール、カウンターと自動ドア　Reception hall, automatic door

エレベーターホール
Elevator hall

エレベーターホールよりレセプションホールを見る
Looking at the reception hall from the elevator hall

自動ドアよりランチルーム方向を見る
Looking in the direction of the lunch room from the automatic door

ガラスの通路、右側は会議室
The glass corridor, with the conference room on the right

上・右下・右頁：一般事務のワークステーションを囲むようにガラスで仕切られた役員個室が配置されている。
左下：会議室は通常、スティディングウォールにより3室に分けられており、個々のミーティングルームとして使われている。

Upper, lower right and right pages: The directors' offices are built with glass and form separations between the workstations.
Lower left: The conference room is normally separated by modular walls into three separate meeting rooms.

ランチルームは建築の段階からリフレッシュルームとしてオ
フィス部分とは仕切られて、眺めの良いコーナーが確保され
ていた。明治通りを見おろすように窓側にカウンターを設け
たため、ここでしばし仕事を忘れ、気分転換ができるであろ
う。曲線が柔らかな雰囲気をつくっている。
バーカウンターは白大理石とステンレス、桜材によりシンプ
ルでダイナミックなデザインにした。カウンターバックのキ
ャビネットはアルミ製で、そこに仕込まれた光により、ここ
もオフィス同様、クリーンでハイテックな空間となっている。

The lunch room was separated from the office in the architectural
stage, and situated in a corner with a good view of Meiji Boulevard.
The counter is set by the window, overlooking the street, allowing
one to relax and forget about work. The curving lines of the wall add
a soft atmosphere to the room.

The bar counter is made of white marble and cherrywood; the
design is simple by dynamic. The cabinet behind the counter is
constructed of aluminum, offering the same clean, polished feeling
found in the offices.

JMC BUILDING
ＪＭＣビル
MYON DONG-SEOUL
ソウル-明洞

既存のオフィスビルの下層部分のファサードと、１階エントランスロビーの改装である。このビルはアパレルメーカーの所有物件であり、またファッション街の中心にあるため、単なる改装ではなく、この企業のメッセージを発するものとなることが求められた。外装は企業の発展を願い、未来感の強いブルーと白を使い、グラフィカルなデザインとすることでファッション性を強めた。また、建物が通りよりもセットバックしているため、その

前庭が若者の集まるポケットパークとなるよう、川砂利によりグラフィカルなパターンを施し、ランドマークとなる水の流れ落ちる袖壁も設けられている。プレゼンテーションの段階ではさらに、低木とベンチ、モニターテレビを設置し、人と情報の出会う場所として「ＭＥＥＴ」というコンセプトを提案していたが、残念ながらそこまでの理解は得られず、結局看板をとりつけるというありきたりで露骨な表現方法をとられてしまった。

ロビーはエレベーターホールまでの距離があるため、やはりここでも情報との出会いとして、ポスターをギャラリー仕立てでスマートに見せるようにしている。照明はハイライトルーバーとＦＬにより、床の大理石パターンと連動した導線を示す、シャープでスピード感のあるデザインとしている。
このビルのもう一方のサブエントランスでは、同様の外壁にガラス張りのファサードをつくり、正面性を強めている。

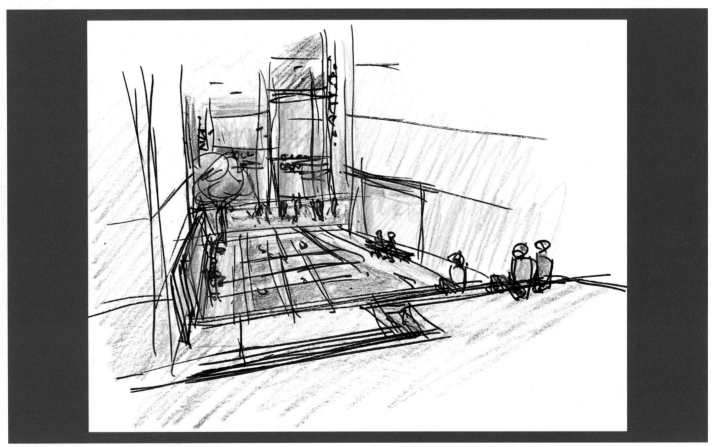

This project consisted of a facade for the building's lower levels and a renovation of the entrance lobby. The building is owned by fashion apparel maker and moreover occupies a central location in the city's fashion district. It wasthe refore requested that the design also project a corporate message. The exterior color of the

building is a futuristic combination of white and blue, and exhibits a graphical design which strengthens its fashion appeal. The building is set back from the street, creating a small "pocket" park where young people can gather. In this square riverstones are laid out in a graphical pattern, and there is also a waterfall cascading

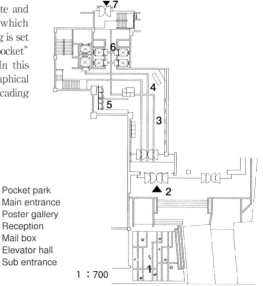

1. 前庭	Pocket park
2. メイン・エントランス	Main entrance
3. ポスターギャラリー	Poster gallery
4. 受付	Reception
5. 郵便受け	Mail box
6. エレベーターホール	Elevator hall
7. サブ・エントランス	Sub entrance

1：700

over the sleeve wall, creating a further attraction. During the presentation we suggested low shrubbery, some benches and a TV monitor, to create an information source location, a concept we called "MEET" but this idea was unfort!unately rejected. Instead, a signboard was installed, and we ended up leaving the frame exposed.

Because of the distance between the lobby and the elevator hall, this area was eventually used for the purpose of providing information, in this case with posters and other art, as a kind of stylish gallery. Illumination includes highlight louvers and flood lights, which cast a sharp light over the patterned granite of the floor, working to create guiding lines and a sharp, speedy feeling.

The building's sub-entrance also sports a glass facade, strengthening the sense of a frontal approach on this side of the building.

プレゼンテーション

ビルの前の空間は「MEET」をコンセプトに、"人と人が出会う""人と情報が出会う"広場として計画した。

広場を構成するのは、低木と噴水、ベンチ、モニターTV　広場性を強調する床のデザイン　広場を見おろす屋外劇場式ベンチ　背景となるビルのファサード、である。

低木と噴水は待ち合わせの目印となるものである。サインだらけの雑踏の中で木

の葉は風を想わせ、水の音は都市のノイズを和らげる。ベンチでは人々が待ち合わせ、会話が始まる。モニターTVは様々な情報とともにこの企業の広告を流すこともできる。広場は川砂利と天然石のコンビネーションによるスペイン的デザインで、企業名のアルファベットも散りばめてある。

階段の一部は屋外劇場風に一段おきになっており、広場を見おろせる。道行く

人々や広場での出会いの風景が両脇のビルにフレーミングされ、ドラマのようである。広場の背景となる本体のビルは、自然なムードの広場とは対照的にブルーと白で強烈な印象を与える。これは広場を囲む他の三面の商業ビルのにぎやかなデザインを受けたもので、企業の強いメッセージを込めている。

Presentation

The space in front of the building was designed as a square for people and people, or people and information, to meet, hence the guiding concept was "MEET".

The layout of the square included small trees, a fountain, benches and a TV monitor, with a patterned deck and theater-style benches which looked down from a height, adding to the sense of a square. The facade of the building formed a backdrop, as well.

Taken together the low trees and benches form a landmark. In the middle of a congested

city even a picture of greenery will evoke a cool breeze; here the sound of flowing water softens the noise of the city. Sitting on the benches, people have the opportunity to talk and trade information. The TV monitors not only provide a variety of information, but function as avenue for corporate advertising. The combination of river gravel and granite in the square is reminiscent of Spain, and the letters of the company name are also scattered about the square.

The steps are built like an outdoor theater, one level at a time,and look down on the square.

People passing by and those meeting in the square are part of the scenery framed by the buildings on both sides, as if in a drama. The main building stands in opposition to the natural mood of the square, with its white and blue exterior giving an impression of intensity. With the three commercial buildings that surround it, the square has a lively atmosphere, creating a strong corporate message.

前庭は規模が縮小され、床パターンと噴水がつくられた。ビルの低層部外壁はデザイン通りブルーと白のコンビネーションで美しく改装されたが、撮影時にはサインが取りつけられている。

The front garden was scaled down, the floor patterned and the fountain built. The exterior of the lower level is finished in a beautiful combination of blue and white. The sign was added just before the photo was taken.

床のラインと照明のラインが導線となっており、エントランスよりエレベーターホールへと導く。右手の壁はスティール製曲面パネルにシルバーメタリック塗装が施されている。上下に照明を内蔵し、間接照明となっている。ポスターは差し込み式でシーズン毎に替えるようになっており、長い通路をギャラリー空間にしている。

The lines of the lighting and floor lead from the entrance to the elevator hall. The wall on the right is steel paneling painted silver metallic. The lightning is built into the wall both above and below. The posters are changed with each passing season, and form a sort of gallery.

改装前は利用率が高いわりに全くの裏口としての外装であったサブエントランスは、エントランスホールを、狭いながらも二層分のガラス張りによる吹き抜けとし、明るく解放感のある空間とした。入口にはキャノピーを設け、正面性をさらに強めている。

The sub-entrance at the rear of the building was used frequently but was nondescript. The new design used a two-story glass facade and open ceiling to transform a narrow space into a bright, spacious interior. The addition of a canopy over the doors adds a further sense of a proper front entrance.

改装前のビルの正面玄関、およびサブエントランス側の外観。地味な外装で、ファッションストリートより後退していることもあり、存在感がなかった。サブエントランスもいかにも裏口といった造りであった。

The front of the building before renovation, and the sub-entrance. This was a plain, retiring exterior for such a fashionable street, offering no presence. The sub-entrance was also no more than a back door.

EBENEZER FASHION MALL

エベネツェル・ファッションモール

MYON DONG – SEOUL

ソウル －明洞

ソウルの中心街、明洞にあるファッションビルのファサードと、1階から3階までのリニューアルである。このビルは韓国のアパレルメーカーがオーナーであり、一部のテナントを除き、大半が自社ブランドにより構成されている。実は3年前にこのクライアントの最初の仕事として1階のデザインをしているので、これについては二度目ということになる。4階部分は2年半前に、ジーンズとカジュアルのフロアとしてリニューアルしており、この部分の改装は今回は見送られた。この3年間に、インポートブランドを除くこのメーカーのほとんどのブランドのショップデザインをし、マニュアルを作成しているので（韓国ではいつもそうなのだが）、仕事の依頼から完成までひじょうに短いスケジュールながら、フロア構成、パブリックデザイン、各ショップのレイアウトがスムーズに進行できた。

デザインはこのメーカーの将来への発展に向け、「未来」をコンセプトに、ファッションビルの環境としては珍しく、シンプルでモダンなものにした。ファサードはブルーとシルバーのコンビネーション（これは同じオーナーのもつJMCビルでも用いられている）によるストライプとすることでスピード感を出している。外壁に取りつけたブラケットランプには、このビルの名前が透かしとなって入っている。

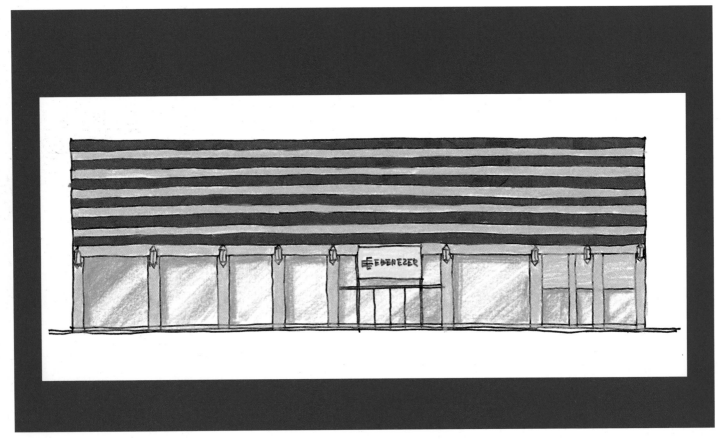

This project was a renewal of the facade and first through third floors of a fashion building in Seoul s central district of Myon Dong.

The building is owned by Korean fashion apparel maker and with the exception on one part of the building, which houses tenants, it is devoted entirely to company brands. Actually, my first job for this client was the design of the first floor, which I did three years ago, so this was my second project here. The fourth floor of the building, which is dedicated to jeans and casual wear, was redone just two and a half years ago, so it was omitted from the plan on this occasion.

During these three years I have produced shop designs for all the apparel brands of this company with the exception of its import brands, and created manuals (always required in Korea), and while the project schedules from request to completion have been extremely tight, we have succeeded in finishing floor layouts, public designs, and each shop layout without delay.

The designs were created to enhance the future development of this maker, and the concept, which is "the Future," is symbolized by the building's very simple and modern environment, which is quite unusual for a fashion building. The coloring of the facade is a combination of blue and silver (which is also used in the JMC building, another company building) in a striped pattern which evokes a sense of speed. The bracket lamps on the outside of the building glow with the building's name.

1. エントランスホール	ENTRANCE HALL
2. エスカレーター	ESCALATOR
3. エレベーター	ELEVATOR
4. 階段室	STAIR CASE
5. ショップ1	SHOP 1
6. ショップ2	SHOP 2
7. ショップ3	SHOP 3
8. ショップ4	SHOP 4

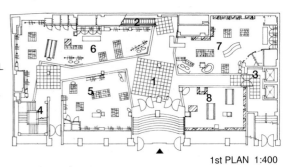

1st PLAN 1:400

通路の交差するところには、白のアクリルルーバーと蛍光灯による大型の照明器具を設けている。そのポイントを明確にするためで、さらに床のパターンと連動させることで小さな広場を形成している。コーナーにより丸や正方形など異なった形を与え、楽しさを出している。

The large-sized illumination fixtures at the juncture of the corridors use white acrylic louvers and fluorescent lamps. In order to make this junction clearer, the floor pattern interacts with the ceiling, creating a small square. The corner positioning allowed the use of both circular and angular designs, producing a lighthearted effect.

メンズブランド MODUS VIVENDI
"大人のための服" に合わせ、黒とチーク材により重厚でメリハリのきいたデザインとしている。

Men's brand "Modus Vivendi"
This modulated design uses black and teak wood to match the "adult apparel."

エレベーターホール：楽譜によるグラフィカルなデザイン
The graphic design in the elevator hall utilizes patterns of musical staff.

40

エレベーター、エスカレーター、階段には上下移動のストレスをなくし、楽しく利用してもらえるような工夫をした。例えば、エレベーターの壁面には楽譜のモチーフを使って音楽を感じさせ、階段はカラフルなアクリル照明で楽しさを演出している。さらに4階のジーンズコーナーへ上がる階段は、イメージ写真をコラージュしたグラフィカルな光壁となっている。エスカレーター脇の壁は、看板用の透過シートを用い、蛍光灯を内蔵した光壁で、サイバーな空間となっている。

The elevators, escalators and stairs were designed to alleviate stress and make travel up and down more pleasant. For instance, a musical staff motif is used on the walls of the elevators, while the stairs are lit with colorful acrylic illumination. Along the stairs which climb to the jeans section on the fourth floor is a backlit wall with a colorful collage of photographs. Along the escalators transparent sheet walls stand as backing for posters and signs. Equipped with internal fluorescent lighting, these walls create a "cyberspace" effect.

ヤングブランドI・N・V・Uは、明るい白の空間にブルーやイエローを散りばめ、ポップミュージックのイメージをデザインしている。

The design for INVU, a brand for the young, evokes pop music with its use of blue and yellow in a cheerful, white interior.

PLUSH

プラッシュ

KUMAMOTO CITY

熊本市

よくブティックをつくるときにクライアントと打合せをすると、「今はこういうデザインは古い」、「ああいう素材はダメだ」などと言われることがある。もちろん流行という存在のもとにファッションビジネスが成立している以上、それを置く器にだって流行というものはある。しかし、洋服をつくる側は次のシーズンに売れる服を考えればよいのだが、店をつくる者は次のシーズンだけでなくその次のシーズンも、5年先のシーズンも使えるデザインを考えなくてはならない。

手法はブランドごとに変わるにせよ、洋服を「見」て「買う」店は明るく清潔で、そこの服の色と素材が正しく確認できる空間でなければならず、そのため商品と接するものも、その背景となるものも、素材・色彩ともにニュートラルなものが最良と私は考えている。

この店はほとんどの部分がアルミで仕上がっている。アルマイトという柔らかい光沢と、パンチングメタルによる半透明のシェルで空間を包むことで女性的なムードにしている。写真で見ると、とてもクールでシャープな空間に見えるが、実際にはそこに色とりどり・種々の素材・形の服が置かれ、それによってこの装置の存在感はあいまいなものに消去され、見せるべき商品だけがふわりと空間に浮かびあがることになるのである。

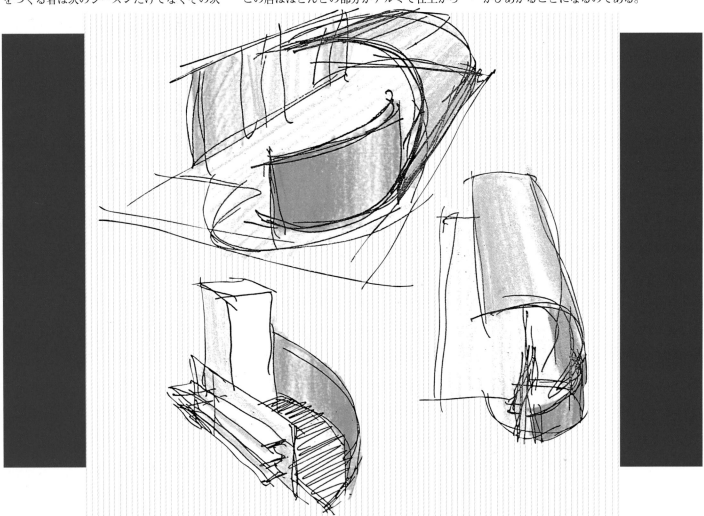

Often when sitting down with a client to discuss the design of a boutique I hear comments like "this kind of design is dated," or "that material is no good." Needless to say, the fashion business is built on trends; it depends on the choice of one item over another. However, while it is fine for apparel makers to focus only on what designs will sell in the next season, for a shop designer it is not just the next season but the one after, and t hose five years from now, that must be considered.

While each brand requires its own unique treatment, apparel is something one sees and purchases, and the shop must therefore be bright

and clean, enabling the shopper to correctly perceive the colors and materials of the products. It is my belief that the colors and materials used to support the merchandise are best left neutral.

In this shop most of the interior is constructed of aluminum. The alumite material has a soft sheen, and I surrounded the interior with a

perforated metal shell that is partially transparent, creating a feminine mood.

The photographs show a very cool, sharply-defined space, but when the interior is stocked with apparel of various colors, materials and shapes, the nebulous quality of the space vanishes and the merchandise floats to the forefront.

1. ウィンドーディスプレイ	WINDOW DISPLAY	
2. 棚	SHELF	
3. ハンガーラック	HANGER RACK	
4. フィッティングルーム	FITTING ROOM	
5. キャッシャー	CASHIER	
6. ディスプレイ	DISPLAY	
7. ストック	STOCK	
8. アクセサリーケース	ACCESSORY CASE	

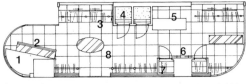

1:200

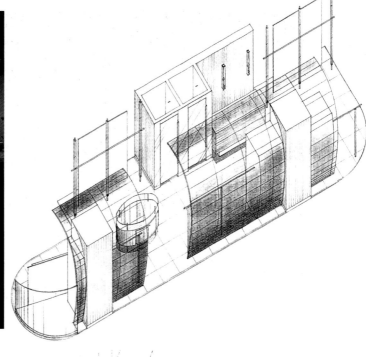

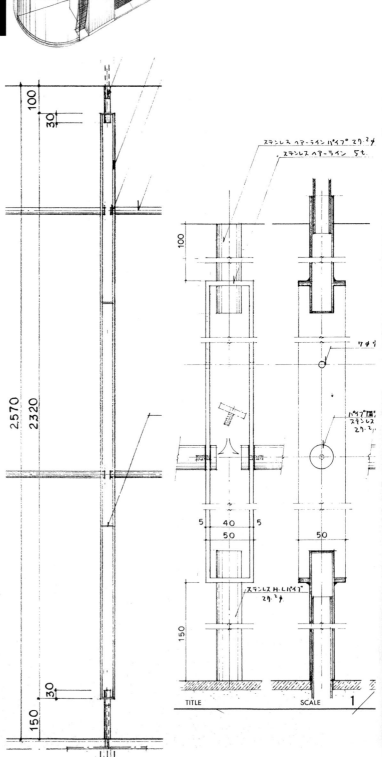

ハンガーラックは商品量に応じて、1段にしたり2段にしたりできるようになっている。支持柱は5mmのステンレスプレート2枚で構成されており、ハンガーパイプは、このスリット内でボルト状のキャップにより固定するというごく単純なものである。この着脱のための機能がそのまま柱のデザインになっているわけである。このデザインはカウンター上のペンダントランプでも繰り返されている。こちらの機能はやはり可変システムであるが、ペンダントそのものが天井高に応じて長さを調節できるようになっている。

Hanger racks are designed to accommodate either one or two rows, depending upon the amount of merchandise being displayed. Two pieces of 5mm stainless plate support the hanger pipe, which is bolted into slits in the arms. The simple device, which allows for quick removal or fixture of the hanger bars, is left exposed as part of the arm design. The same device is used in the pendant lamps on the counter tops. As one aspect of an adjustable system, the length of these pendant lamps can be altered to suit the height of the ceiling.

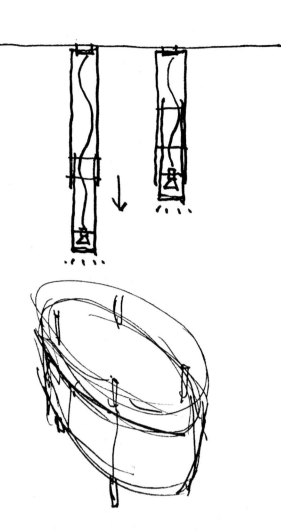

RENOMA HOMME
レノマ・オム
SHIBUYA – TOKYO
東京－渋谷

正統派でありながら、粋やダンディズムのただよう服というコンセプトに合わせ、ショップも計画された。

構成は、ウィンドーをしっかりとり、色、柄、サイズ別に収納できるシャツ棚を設けること、ジャケット・パンツを2段でとり、コーディネートしやすいようにする、そのコーディネートテーブルを設ける、アクセサリーのコーナーを確保する、フィッティングのための充分なスペースをとる、といったヨーロッパのメンズショップの基本に従っている。

しかしその素材はステンレスとチーク材で、さらにつや消しの黒のコンビネーションにより、モダンで男っぽく、強い印象を与えるようにしている。また、家具やドアハンドル、各部ディティールのデザインも特徴あるものとしている。

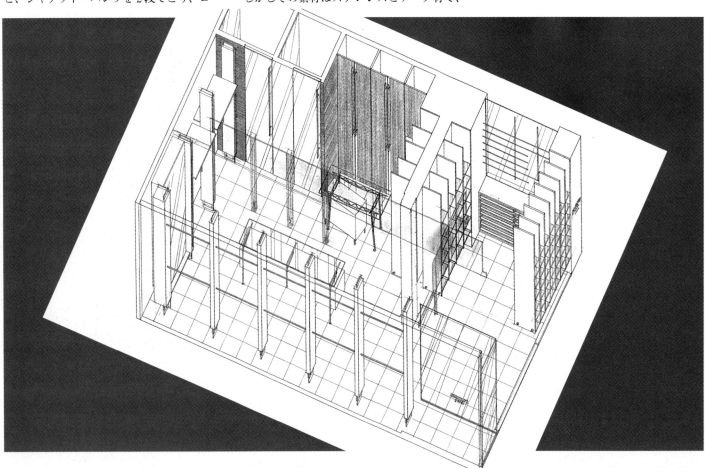

The shop was planned to suit an apparel concept which is basically traditional but also chic and stylish. The layout includes unobstructed windows, shirt racks organized around colors, patterns and sizes, double rows for jackets and slacks, coordinating tables and features accessory corners. This shop, which also provides sufficient space for fitting, is based on the standard European men's shop design.

The materials of the interior are stainless steel and teak wood used in combinations of flat black, creating a strongly modern, masculine effect. Each of the furnishings, including door handles and other details, was likewise designed to enhance the overall effect.

1. ウィンドウディスプレイ　　WINDOW DISPLAY
2. アクセサリーディスプレイ　ACCESSORY DISPLAY
3. アクセサリーケース　　　　ACCESSORY CASE
4～6. ワイシャツ棚　　　　　SHIRT RACK
7. キャッシャー　　　　　　　CASHIER
8. ストック　　　　　　　　　STOCK
9. フィッティングルーム　　　FITTING ROOM
10. アクセサリーケース　　　　ACCESSORY CASE
11. ハンガーラック　　　　　　HANGER RACK

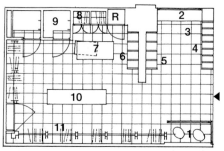

1:200

COMPOSITION 1. — WALL

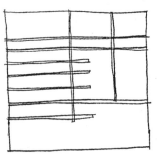

COMPOSITION 2 — window

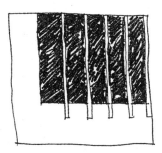

COMPOSITION 3 — ceiling

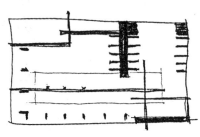

composition 4 — elevation A

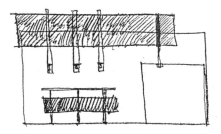

composition 5 — elevation B

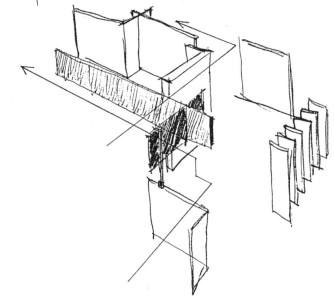

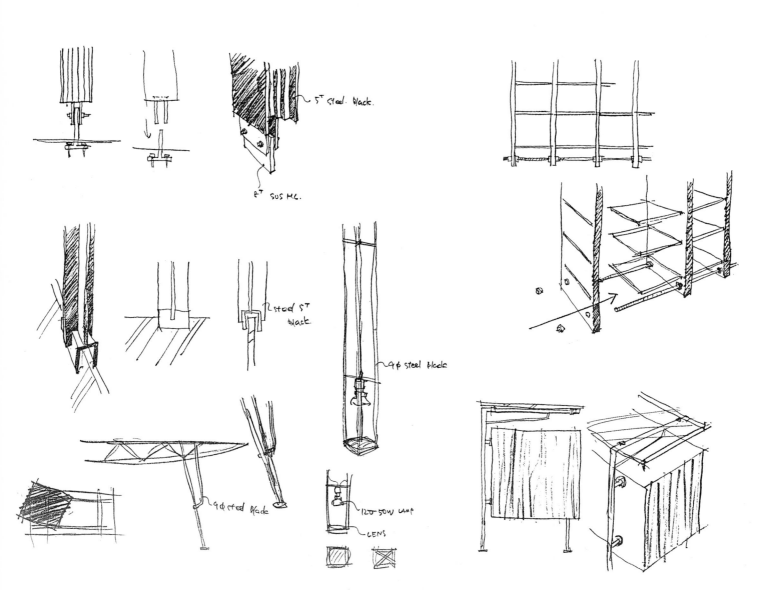

ニット棚やシャツ棚、ハンガーラック、キャビネット、家具等、どの部分も、ステンレス、ガラス、チーク材、黒、グレーのいくつかで構成されている。さらにこれらのコーナーも天井の掘り上げと黒のパネルにより、それぞれが連続し、関係づけられ、立体的にも構成された空間となっている。ひとつの画面に複数の素材を用いるのは、大人のキャリアの幅、人格の幅を表すものであり、また厚い固まりの壁はどっしりとした風格を表し、繊細さを表現するために細い線がディティールに繰り返し使われている。

Knit and shirt shelves, hanger racks, cabinets, furniture - all shop elements are built of combinations of stainless steel, glass and teak, in colors of black or gray. These furnishings are consistent with black panels in the corners and ceiling concavities; continuity and relationships were coordinated in a three-dimensional layout. The appearance on one screen of several materials implies the breadth of an adult career and character, while thick wall sections suggest a settled ambience, and repetition of detailing in fine lines expresses sensitivity.

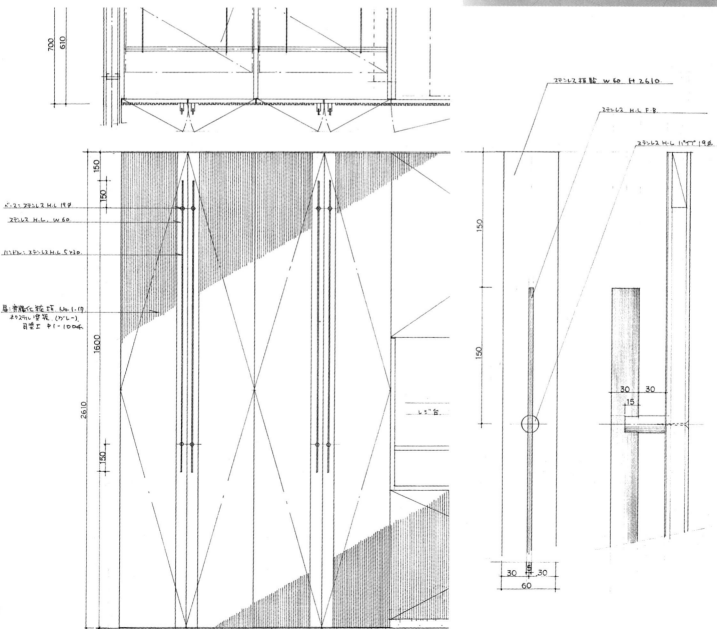

RENOMA HOMME
レノマ・オム
HIROSHIMA CITY
広島市

小さなビルの1階に計画されたショップである。建物が道路よりセットバックしていたため、ウィンドウのみを前面にせり出させ、さらにその上部に照明を仕込んで存在を強調し、認知しやすくした。

空間は間口が狭く、奥で多少広くなっている

ため、キャッシャーを入口側に設け、奥のスペースだけでもゆったりした空間になるようにした。

また天井も低く、空間そのものを見せ場にすることが難しいため、家具やディティールのデザインにエネルギーを注いだ。これらを5㎜

のスティール板を基本素材として作ることをデザインのルールとし、空間の統一感を図りながら、それぞれについては新しいスタイルを追求している。

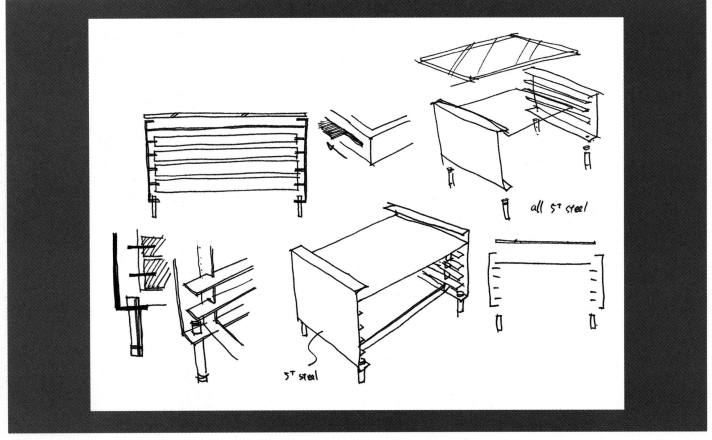

This shop was designed for the first floor of a small building. Because the building is set back from the street, the front display window was extended outward, and fit with ceiling illumination to emphasize its presence.

The shop's entrance is narrow, but there is a little more space in the rear, so the cashier was situated by the entrance, leaving the rest of the shop with more room to maneuver.

The ceiling is also low, making it more difficult to create a sense of space, and requiring that extra care be given to the design of furniture

and details. Using 5mm stainless plate as the basic material of the interior a unified effect was planned, with new styles created for the various elements.

1. ウィンドウディスプレイ	WINDOW DISPLAY
2. キャッシャー	CASHIER
3. ストックルーム	STOCK ROOM
4. フィッティングルーム	FITTING ROOM
5〜7. 棚	SHELF
8. コーディネートテーブル	CO-ORDINATE TABLE
9. アクセサリーケース	ACCESSORY CASE
10. ハンガーラック	HANGER RACK

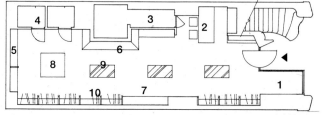

1:200

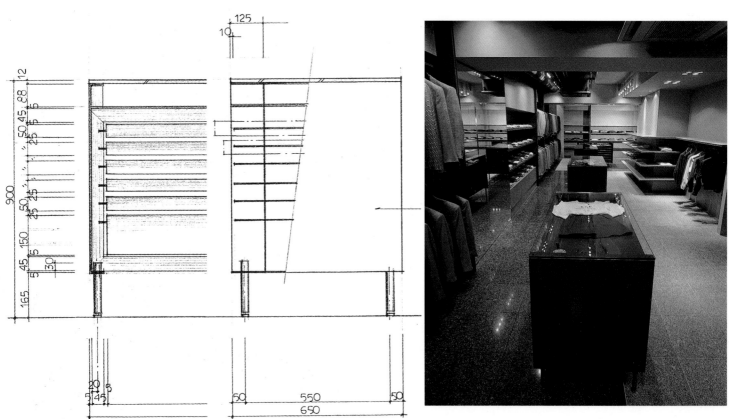

アクセサリーケースは、トップのガラスと引き出しだけが木製である。5 mmのスティールフレームに溶接した、やはり5 mmの桟に引き出しを差し込んだだけの、一切の装飾を排したものである。ブラケットランプは、5 mmのフラットバーを2本の6 φのパイプで支持しているだけの、やはりミニマムなデザインである。

Only the glass top and wooden drawer of the accessory case are not made of steel. With the drawer shut into the 5mm welded steel case there is no visible ornamentation at all. The bracket bars, supported by two 6mm diameter of pipe, are likewise minimized designs.

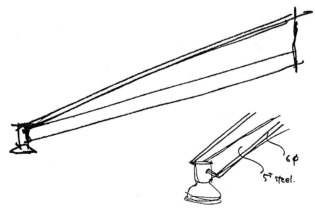

RENOMA WORLD
レノマ・ワールド
SHIZUOKA CITY
静岡市

"レノマ" ブランドのメンズ、レディース、子供服、ゴルフウェア、アクセサリーを集めた複合ショップである。それぞれを明確にコーナー分けし、別々の特徴をもたせながらも、全体的な統一感を図り、一つの大きなショップに見せなければならない。また、間口に対して奥行きが深いため、五つのコーナーの配置と導線が難しい空間である。

入口はビルに既存のものである。まず入口を入り、すぐに五つのコーナーすべてが目に入って、店内の構成を把握しやすいようにした。また、コーナーを分ける壁についても、軸をずらしたり、曲げたりすることで、それぞれの空間に変化をつけている。また、床のパターンや浮かせた棚、照明等により、移動につれて場面がダイナミックに展開していくようにしている。

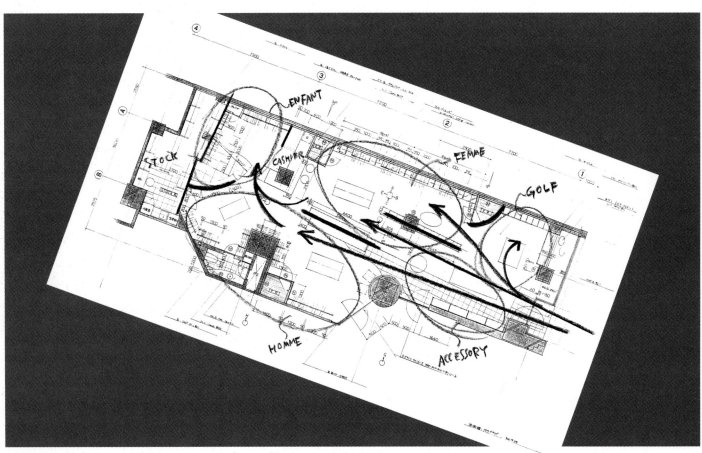

Renoma World is an integrated shop offering men's, women's, children's and golf apparel, as well as accessories. The shop maintains a unified character while featuring clearly defined corners for different products - a requirement in this large space. Moreover, the shop is quite deep from entrance to rear, making the positioning of the five corners and isles a challenge.

The entrance to the building remains in its original form. After entering the shop one immediately sees the five corners, and quickly grasps the layout of the shop. The walls separating the sections can be moved or bent in different ways, allowing for easy alteration of the layout at any time. The patterned floor, floating shelves and moveable lighting make for a dynamic space which can be developed as desired.

1. ウィンドウディスプレイ	WINDOW DISPLAY	
2. ソファ	SOFA	
3. シューズ棚	SHOES SHELF	
4. フィッティングルーム	FITTING ROOM	
5. ハンガーラック	HANGER RACK	
6. シャツ棚	SHIRT RACK	
7. シャツケース	SHIRT CASE	
8. 棚	SHELF	
9. アクセサリーケース	ACCESSORY CASE	
10. ストックルーム	STOCK ROOM	
11. キャッシャー	CASHIER	

1:300

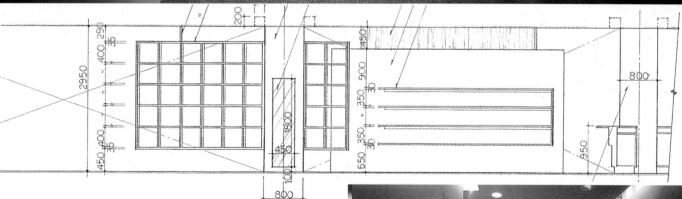

空間に変化をもたせるため、壁やスクリーンの角度をそれぞれずらしている。また、ニット棚やシャツ棚についても、浮かせたり、天井から吊ったりして立体的にもリズムをつけている。

In order to add variation to the space the walls and screens are adjusted at different angles. The knit and shirt shelves are floating or hung from the ceiling, adding a further three-dimensional rhythm to the interior.

ENTREE
アントレ
NAGOYA CITY
名古屋市

現場は、ファッションビルへの地下鉄駅からの入口に位置するハンカチと雑貨ショップである。商品の量・種類とも多く、またそれぞれが色をもっているため、このタイプの店では従来、什器のデザインやディスプレイのシステムがデザインの解答とされ、空間はその配置により決定されてしまっていた。だがここでは、あくまでも魅力ある空間をつくるこ

とを主題とし、商品ディスプレイという機能は二義的なものとして、後まわしにした。
デザインに必要な要素は、目的の違う什器や商品が視覚的にぶつかり合わないように間仕切る機能だけである。配されたスクリーンは、雑多な商品の色を殺すために、それに勝つ色を与えた。また、それぞれが別々の色をもつことにより自己主張し、対立し、重なり合う。

重なり合うスクリーンはまた別の色を生み、新たな対立を発生させる。対面するスクリーン間に生ずる空間と力は、それぞれの動きの中で伸縮増減し、全体では一層大きなパワーを内包することになり、外より内へ入り込む力、内から外へ押し出す力と拡大される。

This handkerchief and accessories shop is located in the basement at the subway entrance to a department store in Nagoya City. Because there are many colors and different items, in the past the layout of this type of shop was determined by the designs and display systems of the items themselves. In this case the attractiveness of the shop interior was given priority over the individual displays, which were decided later.

When designing a space for the display of furnishings and products with different purposes the key requirement is that the items not clash. Here the screens used to separate products were given colors that neutralized that diverse colors of the products. With so many different colors the products stand out, oppose each other, and overlay each other to create new colors. When the screens add to this overlaying of colors they

too create new colors, adding new oppositions to the content of the interior. The space and power created by the opposing screens and their adjustment - through expansion or contraction, growth or diminution - increases the overall power contained in the space between them, drawing in or pushing out with a greater degree of force.

1. ハンカチディスプレイ	HANDKERCHIEF DISPLAY
2. キャッシャー	CASHIER
3. 棚	SHELF
4. ハンカチ棚	HANDKERCHIEF SHELF
5. 傘入れ	UMBRELLA BOX

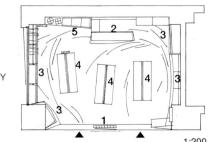

1:200

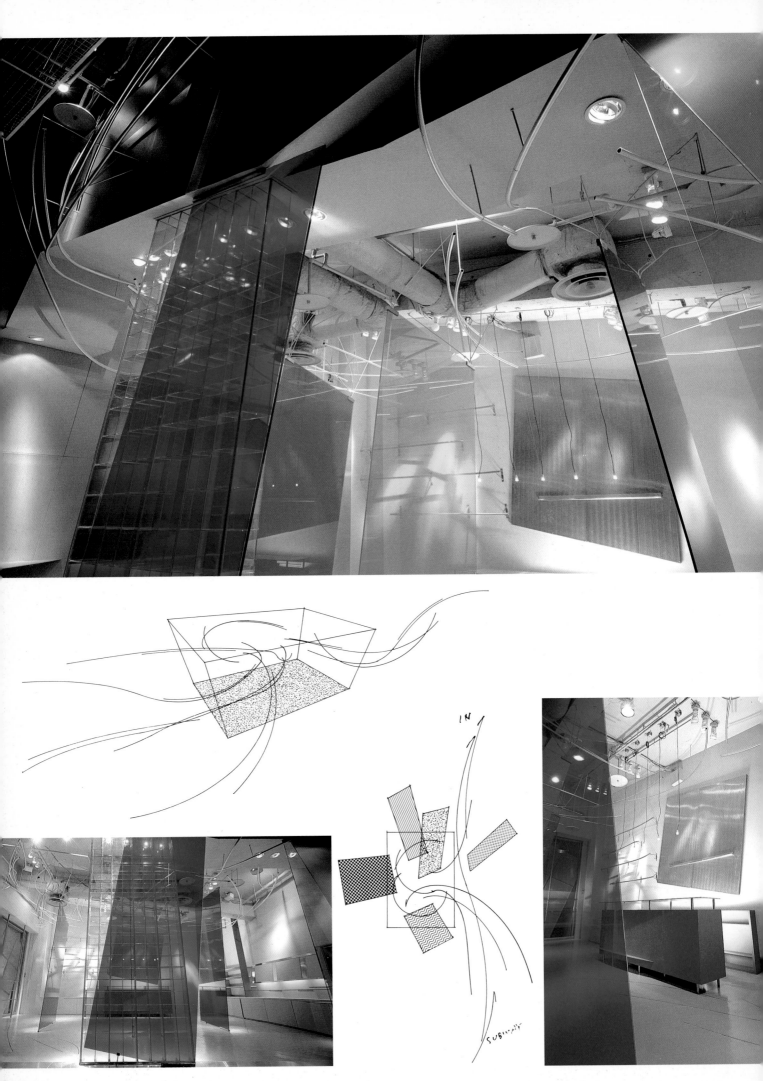

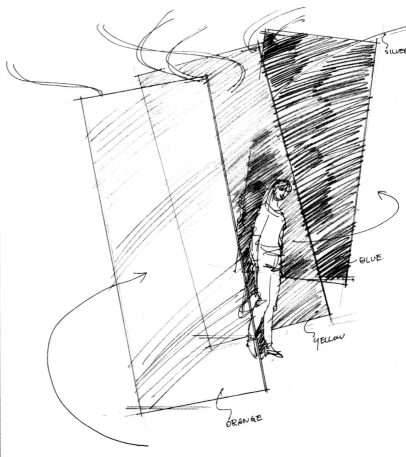

カラーガラスのスクリーンは、クリアガラスに透過性のカラーフィルムを貼っただけのものである。これは、ディスプレーの変更にともない、このスクリーンの色も簡単に変えることができるようにしたもので、店の壁の塗り替え以上に容易で効果的なイメージチェンジを図ることができる。今までの建築＝固定であった概念に対し、"着脱"という考え方を持ち込むことで、"変化できる建築"を提案している。

The colored glass is created simply by applying translucent color film to plain glass. In this way the color of the glass can be changed to fit the nature of the product being displayed quite easily - certainly more easily and effectively than by repainting the walls. In contrast to the traditional notion of architecture as something fixed, this "wear and remove" thinking allows for a new concept, i.e. "changeable architecture."

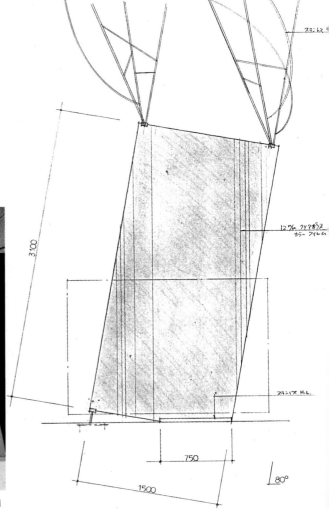

プレゼンテーション用模型　Presentation model

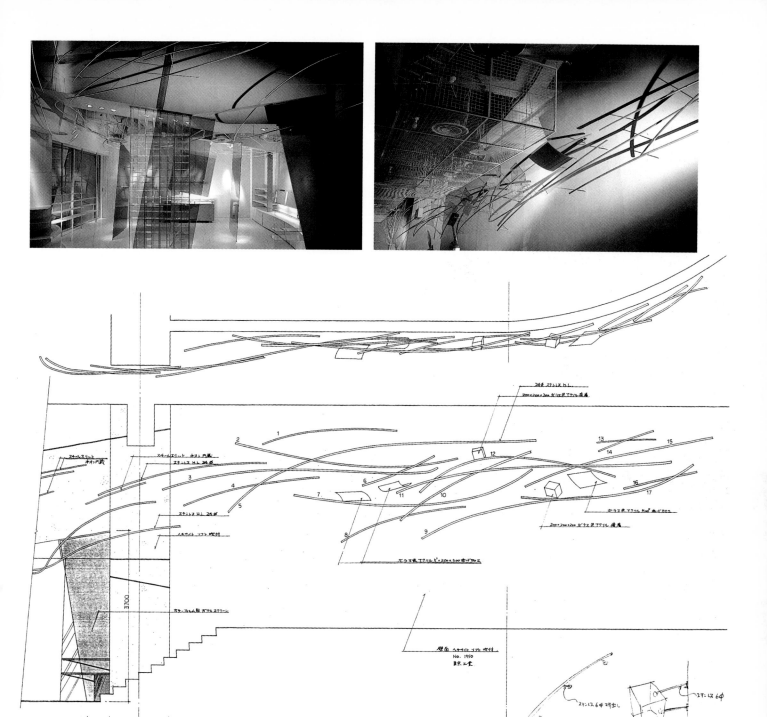

空間に入り込んだ流れは、再び外にあふれ出る。そして
さらに勢いをもって進む。この流れの表現には、24φの
ステンレスパイプが用いられている。図面により指定さ
れた寸法で工場において曲げられたパーツは、現場でバ
ランスを調整しながら一本一本ていねいに固定された。

The energy that flows into the space flows back out again. It
then proceeds on its way with even greater force. To express
this flow I used 24mm staialess-steel pipe. The measured
lengths of pipe were bent to specifications at the factory, then
carefully assembled, on by one, in the shop.

NISHI STYLES
ニシスタイルズ
OMOTESANDO – TOKYO
東京－表参道

南青山における85㎡の路面店である。ウィンドウショッピングを楽しむ人通りの多い通りに面しているため、当然入りやすい店を計画しなくてはならない。ここでは単に開放的な

ショップではなく、外の都市の状況が中へ引き込まれ、通りのエネルギーが出入りするようなデザインを試みた。
空間には林立する高層ビル、ネオンサイン、

公園、高速道路といった都市を構成する要素をイメージ化し、配している。客は散歩の連続として小さいながらも抽象化された都市を回遊することになるのである。

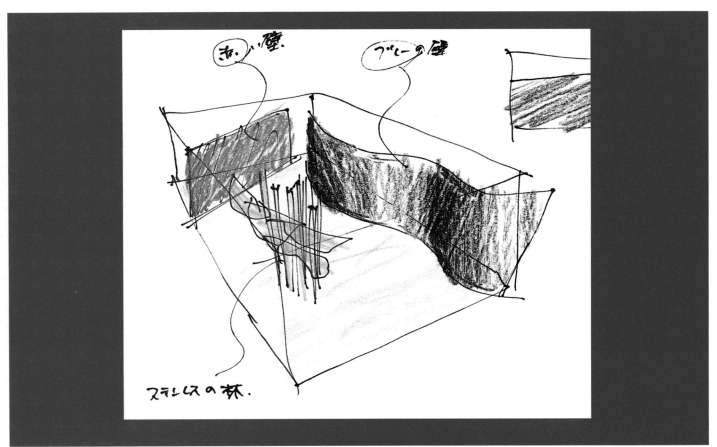

This 85 square meter shop is located in Minami Aoyama in Tokyo In this very popular window shopping area it was essential to design a shop that was easy to enter. But this shop design is not intended merely to have an open feeling; rather, its intent is to bring in the surrounding city, letting the energy of the street flow in and out of the shop.

The shop design takes the forest-like high-rises, neon signs, parks and expressways of the city and uses them as elements of its theme. The shop interior thus allows pedestrians who enter it to continue their stroll through a scaled-down abstraction of the city itself.

1. ハンガーラック	HANGER RACK
2. ガラス棚	GLASS SHELF
3. アルミ棚	ALMINUM SHELF
4. フィッティングルーム	FITTING ROOM
5. ストック	STOCK
6. キャッシャー	CASHIER
7. コーディネートテーブル	CO-ORDINATE TABLE

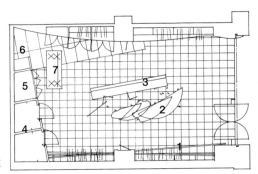

1:200

ステンレスの杯.

雲の よろる

変形のガラス棚、アルミの直線の棚、スカーフ用のディスプレイ・バー、この三つがランダムな柱によって支持されている。商品を置くまでその機能が分からないような、美しいオブジェとして空間の中央に設置されている。風景を抽象化しているため、クリーンで硬質な素材ながらも、何となく以前に見たことがあるような不思議な感覚が、あとで心に残ってくれるのではないだろうか。

Differently shaped and oddly arranged glass shelves, linear aluminum shelves and scarf displays are the central focus of this shop design. Without merchandise it would be difficult to perceive the purpose of the arrangement, except perhaps as an objet d'art. Beautifully set in the middle of the space, it is created of clean, simple materials. It leaves the lingering and rather strange impression of something seen before.

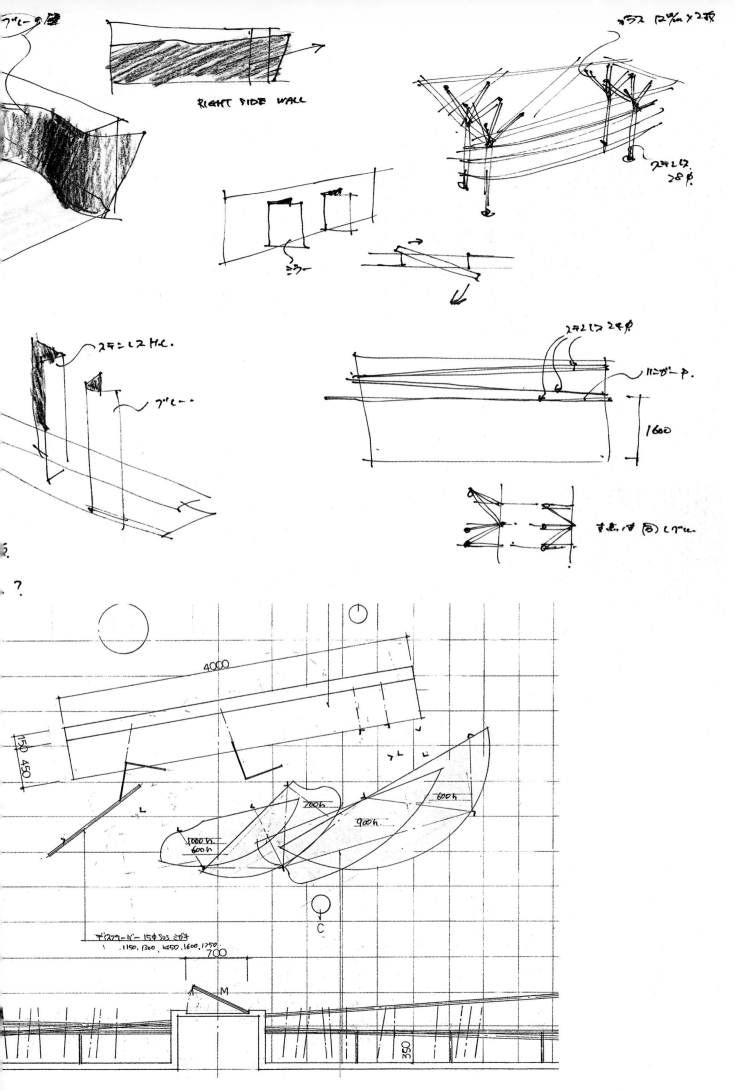

RIGHT SIDE WALL

NOIVAN STEIN
ノイバンシュタイン

ATSUGI CITY – KANAGAWA
神奈川県 – 厚木市

40代ミセスをターゲットにしたブティックである。クライアントからの条件は、白木をアクセントに、全体としては白い空間をつくることである。
条件は非常に簡単なようだが、白い空間というのは、限られた予算ではチープなものになりやすく、さらに白木の処理を誤ると、若年層向けのカジュアルなものになってしまう。

さらに打合せの中で、クライアントがオーソドックスでシンプルなレイアウト表現を好むことが分かった。
結局デザインは、導線と機能から正攻法に進め、ディティールにより空間をひきしめ、高級感を出すこととした。
このディティールにはステンレスを使い、クライアントの条件である白と白木の意味を際

立たせた。また、ブランドのアイデンティティーをも持たせられるよう、ボリューム、厚さ、ジョイント方法等に気を使った。
ブティックの顔となるウィンドーには、とりわけキャラクター性をもたせるため、白木を使った彫刻的な見せ場をつくった。

This boutique attracts ladies in their forties. The client wished to place accent on the white wood, and white was thus chosen as the overall color of the space.

The conditions may seem simple, but in fact a white space done without a good budget runs the risk of looking cheap. Moreover, a misstep with the use of white wood could result in a "young casual" shop effect.

On top of this, it became clear during the discussions that the client preferred an orthodox and simple layout.

It was finally decided that we would pursue a straightforward method based on lines and functions, polishing the detailing to create a highly refined feel.

For the detailing we used stainless steel, going to great lengths to achieve the client's demand of white wood on white. At the same time, to satisfy the brand identity requirements of the merchandise, we used a joint method and other techniques to bring out volume and thickness.

The front window is the face of the boutique, and therefore to give this area a certain amount of character we added a sculpted effect to the white wood display area.

1.	ウィンドウディスプレイ	WINDOW DISPLAY
2.	ハンガーラック	HANGER RACK
3.	ニットケース	KNIT CASE
4.	アクセサリーテーブル	ACCESSORY TABLE
5.	棚	SHELF
6.	フィッティングルーム	FITTING ROOM
7.	カウンター	COUNTER
8.	ストックルーム	STOCK ROOM

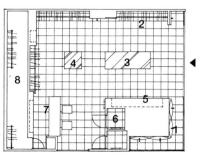

1:200

このブティックの顔となるウィンドウには、一目でこのブランドと分かる特徴のあるデザインが求められた。

与えられた要素は、白と白木である。

従ってウィンドウには、白木材を用いて、商品のブランド・コンセプトと共通性があり、なおかつ他のショップとの差別化を図ることができるような見せ場がなくてはならない。

私は、白木というありふれた素材の既成概念を裏切るようなデザインを着想した。

・シンプルで直線的な店全体とは対照的に、柔らかでエレガントな女性的ライン

・風にたなびくスカーフのようなイメージ

・ふわふわっと軽快で、ちょっとボリューム感があって優しいミセスのイメージ

このようなイメージを表現するべく、柔らかく波打つ白木のオブジェとなった。

このオブジェの製作には、むくの板材ではなく、下地にスティールが使われている。柔ら

かなラインを自由に出すことができることと、軽く風になびくスカーフのようなイメージを出すためには、極力薄くしなければならず、なおかつ長期使用にも型崩れしない強度が必要とされたからである。また、それぞれのパネルを点でジョイントできることも大事な要素であった。こうして、この厚さ1.6mmのスティールで製作されたオブジェに天然木シートが貼られることになったのである。

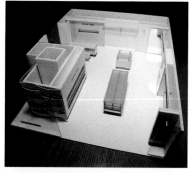

模型写真
Model photo

A design that made the quality of the brand instantly recognizable was required for the front display window, or "face," of this boutique.

The only elements to work with were the color white and white wood.

The task was to create a display using white wood in a way that related to the concept of the brand, while at the same time distinguishing this location from other shops.

I decided on a design which betrayed the existing notions of how white wood could be used.

In contrast to the simple overall layout of the shop, I aimed at soft, elegantly feminine lines:

A scarf blowing in the breeze.

And easy-going and light-hearted, but slightly voluminous image suitable to an elegant lady.

The result was these softly undulating wooden shapes.

In order to create these wood objects, the underlying material needed to be steel, not wood. This was necessary to create light, free lines, like a scarf blowing in the breeze, to make the panels extremely thin and yet guarantee that they could be formed, and to insure that they were strong enough not to deform over long periods of time. This was also very important when building joints at certain points, and because it enabled us to attach the natural wood sheet to the 1.6mm steel panel which we used.

工事中の現場
天然木シートが貼られる前のスティールオブジェ

Site while under construction. The steel objets as seen before gluing of the natural wood covering.

K-HOUSE
K邸
AOYAMA – TOKYO
東京－青山

1フロア約23坪の3層からなる住宅である。1階は応接間で、小さなバーが設けられている。一部可動の間仕切りにより、ゲストルームとして使用できるようになっており、その

ためのシャワールームもある。2階がリビンググルームとダイニンググルーム、キッチン、浴室である。キッチンとダイニングはキャビネットで、ダイニングとリビングはテレビを収

納した壁で仕切っている。各コーナーは明確に分かれながらも、曲面壁により空間は一体化している。3階には寝室が二部屋設けられている。

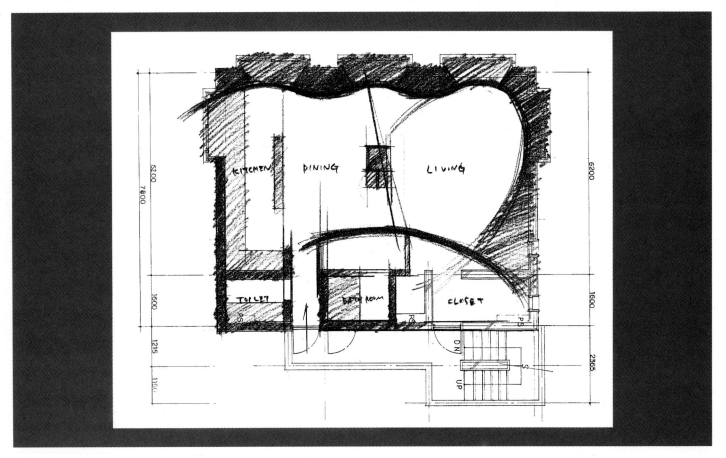

This is a three-story house with each floor measuring about 76 square meters. The first floor is a sitting room and a small bar, but can also be turned into a guest room through the use of a moveable partition, and therefore also

contains a shower and bathroom. The second floor is a living room, dining room, kitchen and full-sized bathroom. The kitchen and dining room share the multi-use cabinets, and the dining room and living room share the TV cabinet. While each

corner has its own clear identity, the curved walls lend unity to the space. There are two bedrooms on the third floor.

1. 洗面所	TOILET
2. 風呂	BATH ROOM
3. 洗濯室	LAUNDRY ROOM
4. キッチン	KITCHEN
5. ダイニングルーム	DINING ROOM
6. リビングルーム	LIVING ROOM
7. 収納	CLOSET

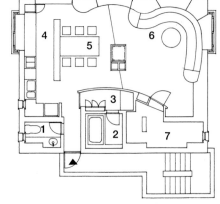

2 nd FLOOR PLAN 1:200

上. 2階、リビングルームよりダイニングルーム、キッチンを見る。
　ダイニングルーム、キッチン側はフローリング、リビン
　グルーム側はカーペットになっていて、二つのコーナー
　分けを明確にしている。
左. ダイニングルーム
　テーブル及びカウンターはサクラ材でできている。

Above : Looking toward the dining room and kitchen from the second floor living room.
　The dining room and kitchen both use flooring, while the living room side is carpeted, clearly distinguishing the two areas.
Left : The dining room.
The table and counter are built of cherrywood.

2階は、キッチン、ダイニングルーム、リビングルーム、浴室から成る。
部屋が硬く冷たい空間にならぬよう、窓側の壁は波型にうねらせている。この有機的な壁の対面は、やはり曲面で受けているが、こちらは幾何学的なラインで、空間に安定感をもたらしている。この内側に脱衣場、洗濯室、浴室の機能が収まっている。脱衣場は狭いな

がらも曲面壁という変化のある面白い空間となった。
リビングとダイニングは、テレビとオーディオを仕込んだ小壁でコーナーを分けている。一部向こうが見えたりして、変化のついた本棚のようにし、その存在を軽くしている。リビングのソファは曲面壁に合わせ、作りつけてある。

The second floor is comprised of a kitchen, dining room, living room and bathroom.

In order to keep the bedrooms from becoming hard, cold places the walls by the windows were curved. Opposite this organic surface, the inner walls are also curved, but the lines are geometric, adding stability to the space inside. The inner side accesses the dressing room, washroom and bathroom. While narrow, the dressing rooms are

also curved, creating an interesting space.

The corners of the living and dining rooms are separated by a cabinet containing TV and audio components. The opposite sides can be seen as if through a bookshelf, lending a light sense of the presence beyond. The sofa in the living room is built to fit into the curved wall.

2階リビングルーム
曲面の壁に合わせて作られたソファが空間に流れと柔らかさを与え、家族の自然なコミュニケーションが生まれる。
照明は空間の中心を明確にするように設けられ、家族の心がひとつになるよう意図している。蛍光灯はいっさい使わず、意味もなく明るくすることなく無駄を省き、ぎりぎりに制御している。

Second floor living room
The sofa in the living room adds flow and softness to the living room, making it a natural place for the family to communicate.

The illumination is designed to clearly establish the center of the space, and is intended to unify the family spirit. No fluorescent lamps are used at all, and neither is anything lit too brightly or unnecessarily.

1階は応接室である。濃いグリーンのアクセントカラーを壁の一部に施し、やはりグリーンのカーペットを敷いた、ソファのある落ち着いたコーナーと、床を50mm上げ、ベージュのカーッペトと桜材を壁にアクセントとして使ったコーナーから成る。

床の上がったコーナーは、必要に応じてゲストルームとして使用できるようになっている。通常は壁の中に収納されて見えないが、可動式の木製間仕切りでしっかりと部屋が二分される。パネルは格子の凸凹が施されていて、仕切られた状態でも、仮設の間仕切りには見えないようになっている。また、ゲストのためのシャワールームが設けられている。

The first floor houses the sitting room. A dark green is used as accent on the walls, and there is also green carpeting. In one corner is the sofa, ad ding a settled ambience to the interior, while another 50 sq. meter area of the room is carpeted in beige, with cherrywood finishing on the walls.

The corner with raised flooring can be converted into a guest room when necessary.

The wooden separation doors are normally hidden in the wall, but can be rolled out to completely separate the two areas. The paneling is made of a convex-concave lattice, but still blocks the view of the opposite side when in use. There is a shower room for guests, and the sitting room can also be used for parties.

There is a compact bar counter for these

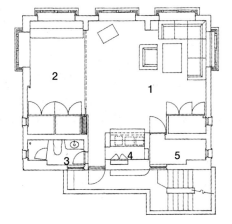

1. ソファ　コーナー　SOFT CORNER
2. ゲストルーム　　GUEST ROOM
3. 洗面所　　　　　TOILET
4. バーカウンター　BAR COUNTER
5. 収納　　　　　　CLOSET

1st FLOOR PLAN 1:200

応接間では簡単なパーティも可能なように、
コンパクトなバーカウンターも備えている。
照明はアッパーライトで地明りとり、一部壁
面に間接照明を仕込み、空間に変化をつけて
いる。他は、テーブル上に最小限のミニダウ
ンライトがあるのみである。

occasions, as well.
　An upper light casts illumination on the floor,
and there is also indirect lighting built into the
walls, adding variation to the interior. Other than
this, there is a small mini-downlight over the
table.

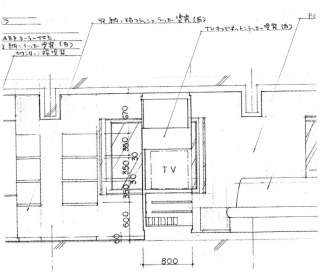

ダイニングルームよりリビングルームの床は90mm上がっている。コーナーの差別化を明確にするためであるが、逆にこの二つのコーナーを曲面壁のコアで一体化し、空間そのものはひとつの大きなものとして感じられるようにした。

The living room is 90mm higher than the dining room. This is partly in an effort to clearly delineate the two corners of the house, but these two corners also form the core of the curved wall, and unify it, giving the entire floor a singularly large feeling.

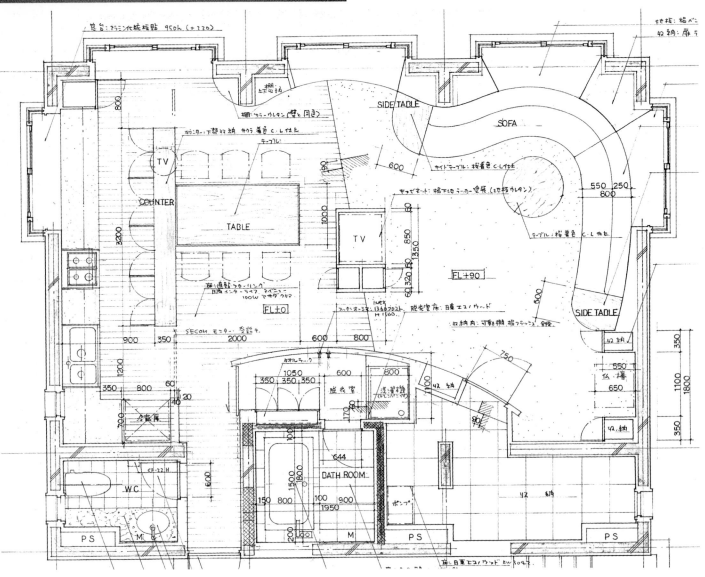

1階のゲストルームは、既存の窓がありきたりにならないよう、手前にサクラ材で仕上げたパネルをつくり、その開口部が窓となるようにした。このパネルには間接照明も仕込まれており、柔らかい光の空間をつくっている。

The first floor guest room has two windows. In order to keep them interesting a cherrywood panel is built over them, opening to reveal the windows. The panel has built-in indirect illumination, as well.

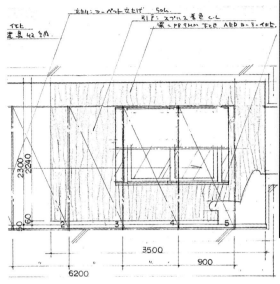

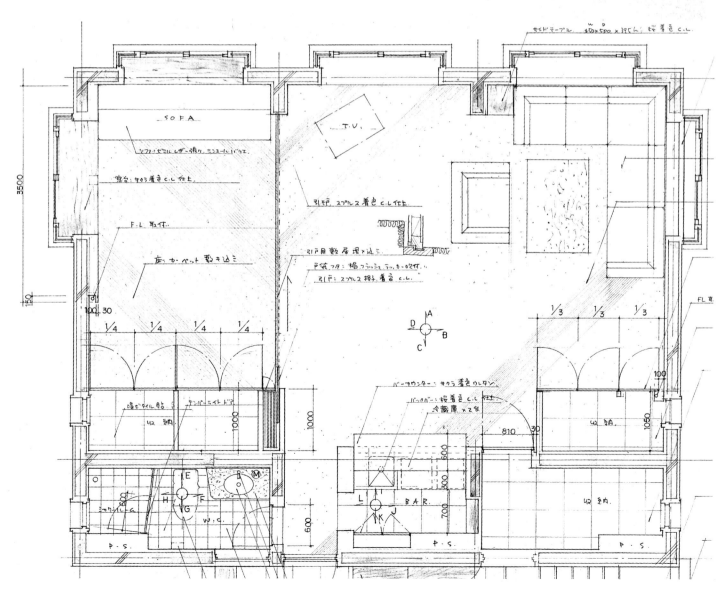

RENDEZ-VOUS CAFÉ
ランデブー・カフェ
NARITA AIRPORT TERMINAL 2
成田空港第2ターミナル2階

空港はとても特殊な場所である。そして国際空港ともなれば、海外旅行が日常化した今日とはいえ、いまだ人々はミステリアスな空気を感じるであろう。それは、柱のない大スパン構造のスペースを見たり、英語のアナウンスを聞いたり、様々な国の人々やクルーが行き交う様子から受けるものである。しかし、今までショップはというと何ら特殊性はなく、デパートの売り場や最上階のレストラン

街と変わるところはなかった。
この「ランデブー・カフェ」の計画にあたっては、空港という特殊性に合わせた空間を創ることをめざした。
ここを利用する人々に「旅の思い」をより大きなものとしてもらうべく、「飛行」をデザインコンセプトとし、結果、近未来のジェット機内、あるいは宇宙ステーションのサロンのようなインテリアとなった。スペース全体

はやわらかな間接照明に包まれ、基本色はグレーでまとめられている。これは未来や科学を象徴する色で、アクセントとして情報を表現するブルーが加わっている。大きくうねる壁は、旅客機の脇を流れる空気を表し、それが未来的フォルムとなっている。また、オープンショップのため、フライト・インフォメーションのアナウンスをＢＧＭとし、タイムテーブルを借景にしている。

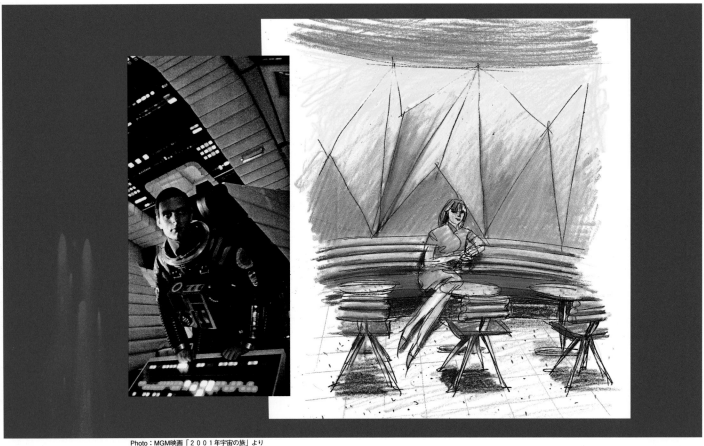

Photo：MGM映画「２００１年宇宙の旅」より

An airport is a very distinctive location. Even today, when traveling to foreign countries is commonplace, an international airport probably affects many people with a sense of mystery. This may be due partly to the huge, column-less interior space, or the announcements in English, or the interactions of the many foreign travelers. But when one thinks of the airport's shops and restaurants, no particular image comes to mind. They generally look like typical department store

appliance floors, or the rooftop restaurantsfound at such locations.

The Rendez-vous Café designed to offer something that could only be created within the unique ambience of an airport.

This concept attempts to go beyond the "idea of travel" to something greater, the "idea of flight," simulating the interior of a near-future jet airplane, or possibly the salon of a space station. The entire interior is enveloped in a soft,

indirect light, and the thematic color is gray, which symbolizes both the future and science. The color blue is added to accent information. The large bending wall is designed as a futuristic symbolization of the air streaming around the fuselage of an airplane in flight. This open shop also borrows flight announcements as BGM, and timetables as backdrop design.

1. キャッシャーカウンター　CASHIER COUNTER
2. カウンター　　　　　　COUNTER
3. 厨房　　　　　　　　　KITCHEN
4. ソファベンチ　　　　　SOFA BENCH
5. メニュー看板　　　　　MENU SIGN

1:200

プレゼンテーション

成田空港第2ターミナルの開港に際して、チェックインカウンター、税関、搭乗ゲート等の基本的機能に加え、レストランや土産物売り場等の周辺施設についても、より良い機能と環境が検討された。

私が設計を担当することになったこのカフェは、日本航空の関連会社がオーナーであるため、とりわけ理想的な形をめざし、日本航空の専任スタッフを中心に何度も会議をもち、企画書を作成した。

現場はアライヴァルエリアにあり、到着客の出てくる1階ゲートの吹き抜けの2階に位置する。従って、ここの利用客は主に出迎え客である。様々な理由で出迎えに来た人々について、ここで起こるいろいろな状況を推測し、それぞれにどのような対応ができるかという方法で、ここに必要な機能を検討していった。

企画書のテーマは「出逢い」。
出迎え客と到着客がスムーズにコンタクトできるようなミーティング・サービス、到着客へのメッセージを伝えたり到着便の時刻を確認したりするメッセージ・サービス、アクセスについての問い合わせを受けたり、リムジンの発券をするサービス等の機能を盛り込んだ企画書がつくられた。

インテリアデザインについては、以上の機能をもつだけでなく、到着客には旅の余韻を、出迎え客には旅に出たくなるような気分にさせる空間とした。

ジェット機の機体を連想させるジュラルミンを使用したり、滑走路を暗示する床のライン、宇宙ステーションのような壁面のオブジェとライティング。ここをフライトの延長部分として、非日常的な空間をデザインした。

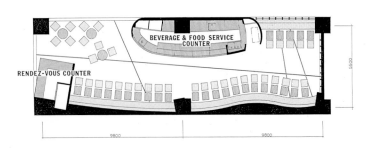

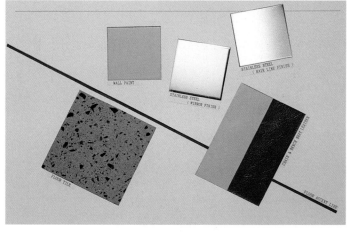

Presentation

When Terminal 2 of Narita International Airport was opened not only the check-in counters, customs, loading gates and other airport facilities were given careful consideration; thought was likewise given to restaurants, souvenir shops and other support facilities, in order to create an ideal environment.

My work here was the planning supervision of this café, which is owned by an affiliate of Japan Air Lines. In order to arrive at the ideal design we held numerous conferences, led by JAL's managerial staff, to develop the proposal.

The location was in the arrival area, on the second floor overlook above the arrival gate exit. Naturally, most of the customers here would be people coming to meet arriving passengers. We considered all the reasons people might be coming here to meet passengers, all the possible situations there might be, and what type of facility would best answer to these needs.

A proposal theme : "Encounter"
Plans which were incorporated into the proposal included services enabling arriving travelers and those greeting them at the airport to make contact without difficulty; messaging for arriving passenger; information on flight arrival times; information on access; and limousine ticketing and other functions.

Above and beyond the functions listed above, the interior design of the café was planned to enhance the sense of travel in arriving passengers, and to instill a desire to travel in those meeting them. The use of duralumin, which resembles a jet fuselage, and runway symbols on the floor, and space age objects and writing as decoration on the walls, were all part of this effort. We created this uncommon interior to be an extension of the flight experience.

設計プロセス

実際の設計に入ると、さまざまな問題が起こってきた。空港のシステム上、ここでコンピューターの端末を使って搭乗者確認をすることができなかったり、リムジンの発券ができないことが分かった。また、第2ターミナルが開港しても、新しい滑走路ができるまでは、利用客数がそれほど多くは望めないということで、一般客をターゲットとしたドリンク中心型から、空港従業員による利用も考え、食事の要素を大きくすることとなった。このため厨房が大きくなり、セルフサービスから通常のオーダー方式に変わった。

空間の素材についても、華やかさを前面に出していた企画書の時よりも、落ち着いて食事ができるよう、ジュラルミンがスティールのライトグレー塗装やカラーガラスへと変更された。

壁はゆるやかにうねっている。この流体力学的なフォルムが、飛行物体内のような感覚を生んでいる。ベンチシートの横リブが、この大きな空気の流れをより明確にしていて、また未来的イメージをも増幅している。これらの基本的デザインは、プレゼンテーション時と同じである。椅子はキャラクター性を強めるため、背と座を切り離した。テーブルについては、上空から見下ろした東京の街をデザインするアイデアがわき、点在する建物を水玉に、道路を線に置き換え、こうして抽象化した2種類のグラフィカルなパターンをシルクスクリーンでプリントした。
また、利用客にメニューを伝えるため、サンプルケースが必要となり、写真により表現することとし、このメニューサインも惑星の軌跡のデザインとなった。

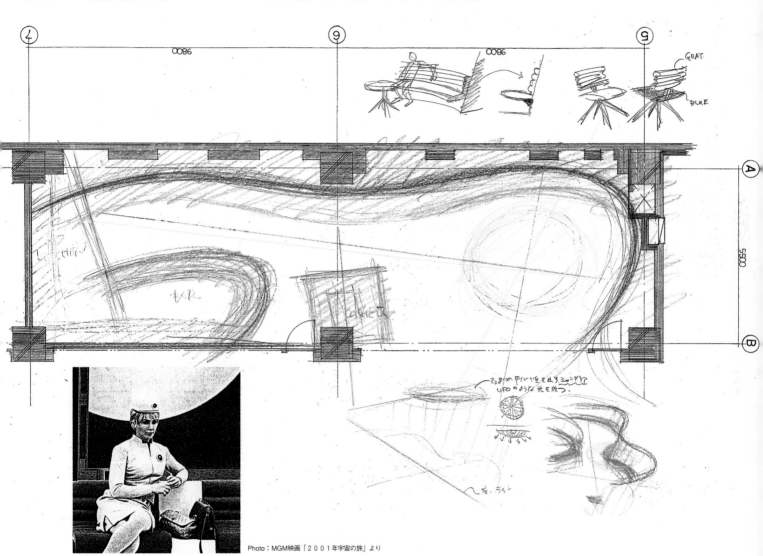

Photo：MGM映画「２００１年宇宙の旅」より

The planning process

When the actual planning began we faced various problems. We found, for instance, that there was no way to confirm passenger arrivals over the computer, and that limousine tickets could not be issued. Moreover, we learned that until the completion of the new runway there would not be a large number of passengers, and that we would be serving more staff as a result, so that it became more important to offer a full menu than to serve mostly drinks. This required a larger kitchen, and a change from a self-service format to regular ordering service.

The elements of the interior also changed.

Where we originally intended a very showy interior, a more subdued space appropriate to eating a meal was now required. We decided to do away with the duralumin, using instead steel, gray paint and colored glass.

The walls are gently curving. This form, which is that of fluid mechanics, gives one the impression of being inside a flying body. The side ribs of the bench chairs add further to the flowing feel of this large interior space, and add to the futuristic image, as well. These design elements were included in the presentation and were used

without change. In order to strengthen the character of the chairs the backs and seats were separated. Then I hit on the idea of making the table tops show a representation of the city as seen from the window of a plane, useing polka dots to symbolize the buildings and lines for roads; these two graphical patterns were then silk-screen printed on to the tables. To present the menu to customers we designed a sample case, laying out photographs of the dishes as if they were planets in orbit.

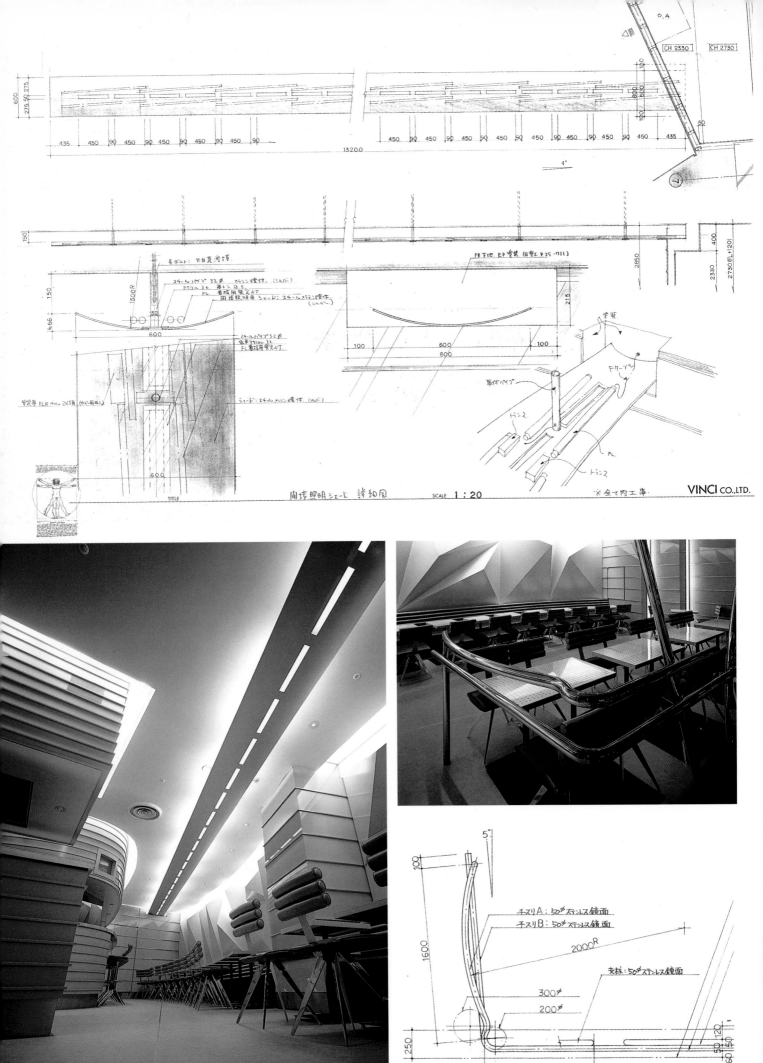

VINCI CO.,LTD.

周接照明シェード 詳細図   SCALE 1:20

手スリA：50φ ステンレス鏡面
手スリB：50φ ステンレス鏡面
2000R
支柱：50φ ステンレス鏡面

空間に合わせ、ロゴ、メニュー、コースター、マッチもデザインしている。ロゴはインテリアのテーマカラーのグレーとブルーを使い、未来的でスピード感のあるものとしている。コースターとメニューに使っている水玉は、テーブルにも使用されている。これは夜間飛行の機内から地上を見おろした時、無限に点在する都市の明かりをイメージしている。

The logo, menu, coasters and matches were all designed to fit the interior space. The logo uses the same interior colors of gray and blue, two futuristic, speedy colors. The polka dots on the coasters and menus are the same as those which appear on the tables. These polka dots are an abstract representation of the site of an infintely expanding metropolis as seen from the window of a plane at night.

椅子も空間に合わせ、未来的なデザインとした。脚はアルミダイカストである。製作をお願いしたアーティック・インターナショナルの協力により、三度の試作を繰り返し、座と背のジョイントの問題、座り心地と微妙なデザイン上のディティール、仕上がりの調整が行われた。強度試験も行い、完璧な形で現場に納められた。

The chairs also a futuristic design made to match the interior. The legs are aluminum dyecast. Manufactured in cooperation with Artech Interational , three trials were required to resolve such problems as the design of the joint between the seat and back, the comfort of the seat, and other fine details of the design. The chairs were also tested for strength before the final product was manufactured for installation at the location.

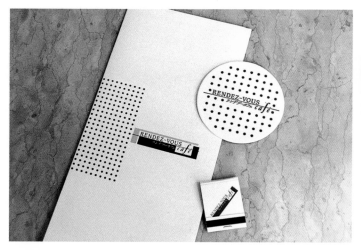

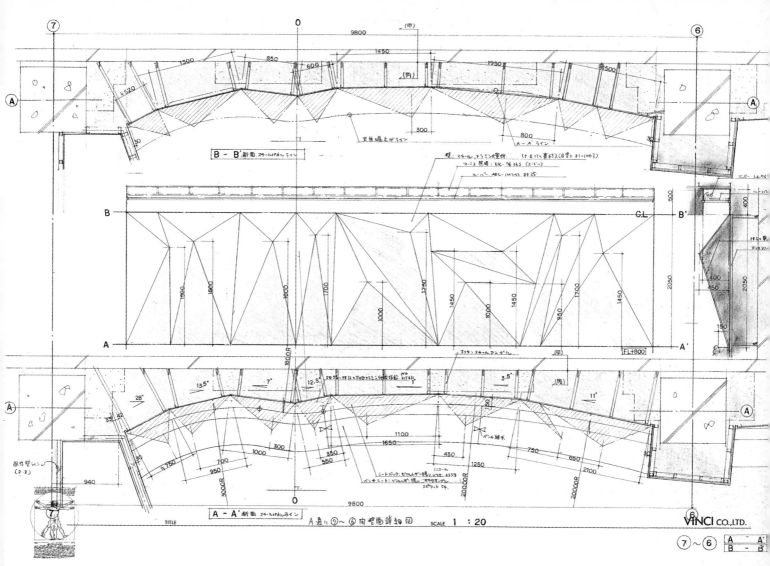

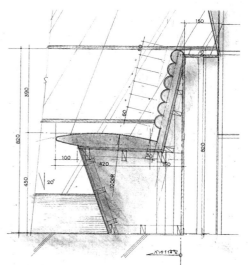

壁面は未来の空港ターミナルをイメージしたもので、間接照明の効果と相まち、さながらSF映画のセットのような趣になっている。シャープな陰影を必要とするため、スティールパネルで全て製作し、ライトグレーの塗装が施されている。壁面がうねっていることと、全て形状の異なるピラミッド型のパネルの組み合わせのため寸分の狂いも許されず、当社で作った模型と図面をもとに、金物工事を担当したブーカーではやはり1/20の模型をスティールでつくり、試作とした。実際のパネルは全くの逃げのない精度を要するものであるため、工場で一たん現場と同様に組み立て、狂いのないことを確かめてから現場に運ばれ、改めて組み立て直され、セットされた。胸のすくような超一級の施工である。

The walls of the interior were created to suggest the interior of a futurisitc terminal, and lit with indirect lighting that was also intended to suggest the set of an SF movie. In order to achieve the desired sharp shadows, everything was constructed of steel panels, which are painted light gray. In order to created the curving wall, which is constructed of differently sized and shaped pyramid panels, the steel contractor had to construct an experiemntal 1/20 scale steel replica, based on the diagrams and models we made at our own office. Because the steel paneling required absolute precision, the entire wall had to be assembled first at the factory. After it was determined that there were no discrepencies, the materials were taken apart and transported to the site, where they were reassembled. This was an extrememly demanding construction project.

JUCHHEIM'S IMBIß
ユーハイム本店・インビス
MOTOMACHI – KOBE
神戸－元町

ここは、かつてカール・ユーハイムが創業した神戸・元町に本店として新築されたビルの地下１階に、１階のケーキ＆グルメショップ、２階の高級ティーサロンとともに計画された、ドイツ風カフェテリアである。

地下への階段は１階の入口より入り、左手にある。階下へ誘導するのは、地下から立ち上がっている巨大なレリーフの壁である。レリーフは様々な立体の組み合わせにより構成さ

れ、これから見る地階の空間の予告編となっている。階段は、床から１ｍほどのところで踊り場を迎える。カウンターと客席との中央に位置し、まずカウンターを確認した客が、階段を降りながらぐるっと店内を見回すこととなる。客席の中央には３本の柱が存在し、空間に安定感を与えるべく天井をしっかりと支え、また店内にリズムをつくっている。この柱や階段脇の壁は、地下を地下としてより

強調することにより、その空間の存在感を印象づけるために、ファーストエスキースの段階から計画されたものである。

神戸の元町というロケーションにおいて、老舗の本店としてのドイツ的風格と気品、なおかつ新しさをも感じさせる空間をつくることができたと思う。

This business was origially established by Karl Juchheim in Motomachi, Kobe, I did the plan for a German-style cafeteria on the basement floor, a cake shop on the first floor, and a luxuarious tea salon on the second floor.

The stairs to the basement are inside the entrance on the left side. A large wall relief invites the visitor to decend into the basement. Therelief is composed of various solid forms, and serves as an indication of what the interior will

present. The stairs end about one meter from the stair landing, which is situated in between the counter and the tables. Coming down the stairs the customer first sees the counter, then winds his way down for a view of the entire shop interior. In the middle of the seating area are three columns which support the ceiling and add a sense of stability, and at the same time a sense of rhythm, to the interior. The columns, and the wall by the stairs, which accentuate the

subterranean location of the space, were ideas that came out in the first sketches of the plan.

At this location in Motomachi, Kobe, I think we succeeded in maintaining the German style and prestige of this old headquarters, while creating a space that makes one feel something new.

1. セルフカウンター	SELF SERVICE COUNTER
2. 厨房	KITCHEN
3. ハイテーブルコーナー	HIGH TABLE CORNER
4. テーブルコーナー	REGULAR TABLE CORNER
5. 洗面所	TOILET

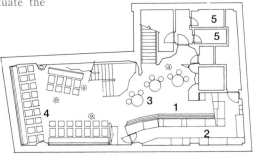

1:300

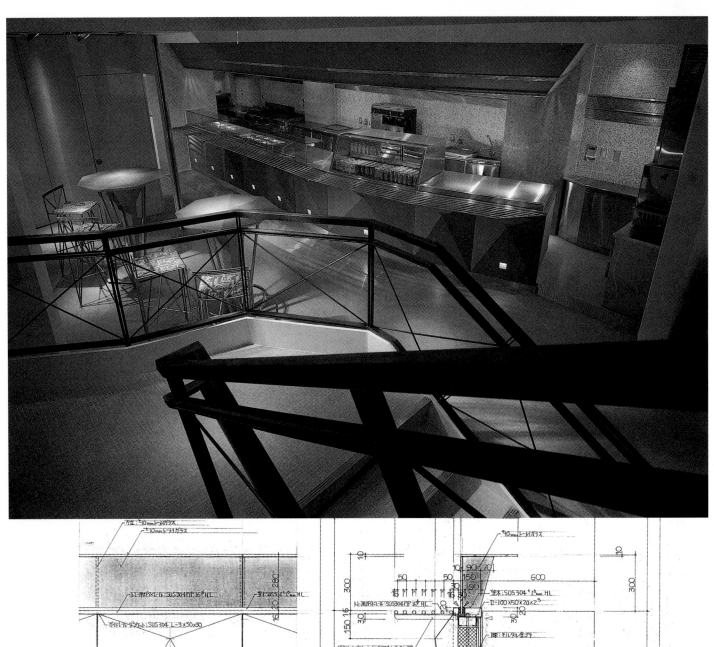

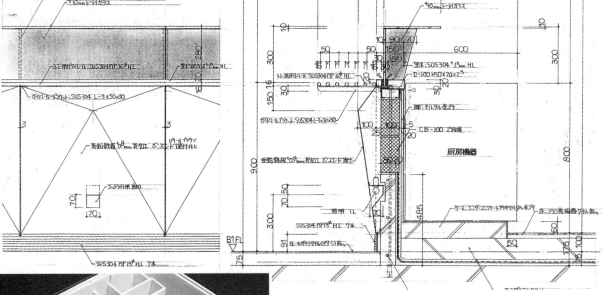

階段を降りてきて、踊り場がほぼ店の中央に位置するようになっている。ここで
サービスカウンターとダイニングルームを左右に見ることができ、空間全体と機
能を認知することになる。デザインは頑強な感じを出すため、キュビズム的な手
法をとり、色も全体に重めにしている。
カウンターの腰部分はスティールパネルに塗装が施されている。幅木とトレイ用
レールはステンレスパイプである。

Decending from the stairs one steps on to the stair lauding, which is
situated in about the middle of the space. From this point one can see the
service counter and the dining room on the left and right, and gain an
understanding of the entire space and its functions. In order to incite a strong
feeling the design employs cubist techniques, including heavy coloring
throughout.

The hip-level portion of the counter is made of steel which is painted
decoratively. The railings for trays are made of stainless steel pipe.

模型写真　Model photo

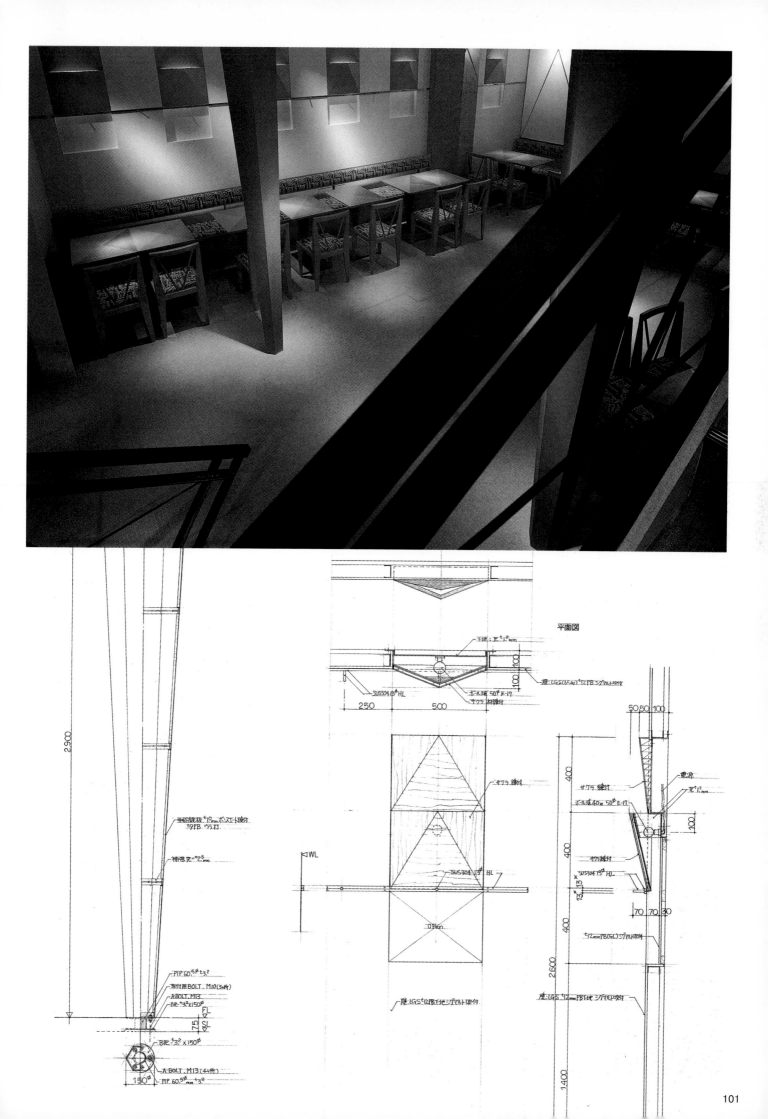

平面図

3本の柱が空間を視覚的にがっちりと支え、安心感を与えている。また、この柱は導線が直線的にならぬよう、空間にリズムを生む役割を果たしている。階段脇の壁は地下空間へと客をドラマチックに誘導するために、様々な形のキュービックで装飾されている。

The three columns create strong visual support for the interior space, also lending it a settled effect. Because the lines of the columns are not straight they also give the space a sense of rhythm. The wall by the stairs, with its varied design of cubic shapes, provides a dramatic approach to the lower level.

LOIS LANE BAR
ロイスレーン・バー
NISHIAZABU – TOKYO
東京 – 西麻布

1階の雑貨と洋服のブティックと同時に計画された、地階のバーである。地階といっても、外からの直接の階段と、中庭のような大きなドライエリアに独立した入口をもっている。1階と地階がそれぞれ独立した空間であるため、吹き抜けに大きな絵を設え、どちらからもこの共通の絵を見ることで上下の空間を一体化させている。

絵は8×8mという壁画のスケールである

が、あえてキャンバスに描き、この吹き抜けのインテリア化を明確にしている。壁画は谷口広樹氏に依頼した。

このバーのコンセプトは、海底に沈んだ古代の宮殿である。劇的な吹き抜けの巨大な絵を見ながら階段を降りていく時間はとても神聖なものであり、入口を入ると再び劇的な空間に出会うことになる。

柱は、タイル、コンクリート、ステンレスに

よる3段の仕上げになっており、時間の経過が表されている。つや有りのモザイクタイルは水を連想させるための素材である。

照明は、天井の高さを強調するため、ペンダントランプを使用している。これは1階のブティックと共通のデザインだが、天井の低い1階のものより、縦長のデザインになっており、空間内でのバランスをとっている。壁面のブラケットランプも縦長のデザインである。

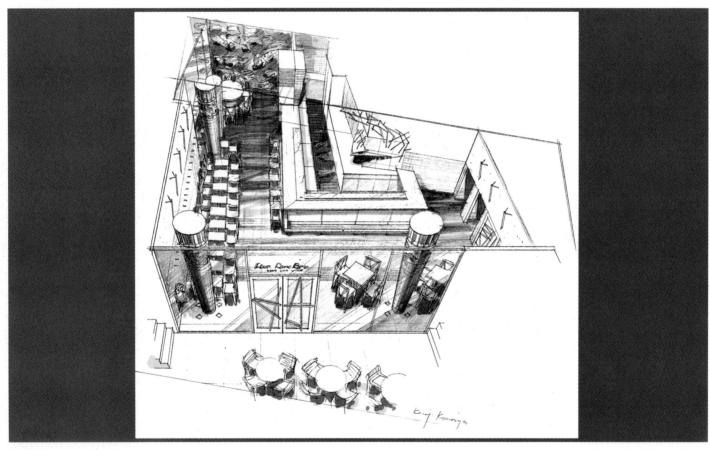

This underground bar was planned at the same time as the first floor apparel and accessory boutique which stands above it. While situated underground, the bar actually has direct access to the street via stairs that lead down into a shared "dry area." Both the lower and upper floor spaces have blown out walls, sharing a view of the dry area's large mural painting which was created by Hiroki Taniguchi. This large painting has the effect of unifying the two floor designs. The painting is 8 X 8 meters, and out of necessity was painted on canvas.

The concept of the bar is that of an ancient

sunken palace. Descending the stairs into the basement one enjoys the divine drama of the huge mural, then enters the bar to a second dramatic scene.

The interior columns, which were created in three stages and are made of tile, concrete and stainless steel, suggest the passage of time. The shiny tile mosaic was created because it creates the illusion of water.

In order to emphasize the height of the ceiling the space was illuminated with pendant lamps. This design is shared with the first floor boutique, but as the ceiling is much higher in the basement,

the design is lengthened vertically for balance. The bracket lamps on the walls also use a vertical design.

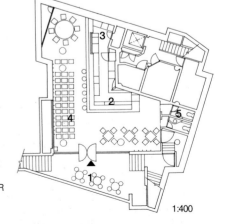

1. 絵　　　　　　　PICTURE
2. バーカウンター　BAR COUNTER
3. キッチン　　　　KITCHEN
4. テーブルコーナー　TABLE CORNER
5. 化粧室　　　　　TOILET

1:400

南国的な解放感のある店である。色彩も土
の色の茶と、ジャングルの葉の緑のコンビ
ネーションとし、ドライエリアの壁の絵の
題材と色彩も店内との調和を図るため、谷
口広樹氏に「猿の記憶」と題するものをお
願いした。ガラス越しに見えるこの絵は、
絵を超えた風景となり、1階にとっても2
階にとっても、豊かで不思議な空間をつく
り出している。

This bar has an open, tropical feeling. The
colors are a combination of earthen tones and
jungle greens. The wall along the dry area is
decorated with the a piece of art by Hiroki
Taniguchi "Monkey Memories," which
supports the interior design with similar
textures and coloring. Seen through the glass,
this landscape transcends the quality of a
painting, lending an otherworldly ambience to
both the first and basement floors.

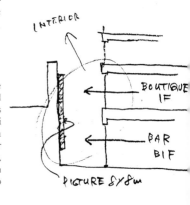

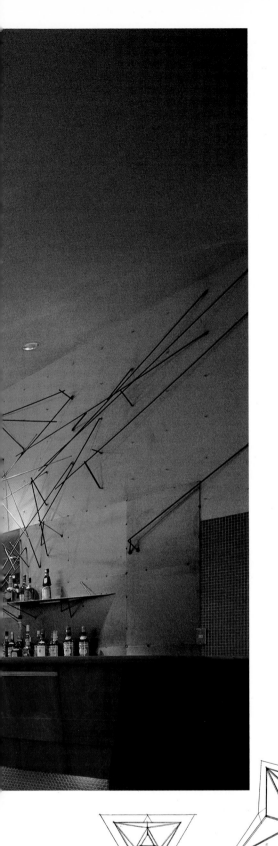

B１F用ランプ　　　　　　　　１F用ランプ　　　　　　1 st FLOOR LOIS LANE BOUTIQUE

REVUE
レヴュー
TSUBAME CITY – NIIGATA PREFECTURE
新潟県－燕市

日本最大のシルバー食器の生産地として知られる新潟県燕市。このショールームは、地元の食器問屋が市内のショッピングセンター内にアンテナショップとしてオープンしたものである。

設計にあたって最初に色を決めた。ナチュラルブラウンとブルーである。前者は、通常の家庭で食器が置かれる木のテーブルの色。日常的な空間を演出するためのものである。一方ブルーは、ひとつひとつの食器のデザインと存在感を強調するための非日常的な背景色として用いている。とりわけシルバー食器を浮き立たせるのにブルーは最適である。各部のデザインは、色の効果が最大限に引き出せるように決めていった。スティールパネル、棚、家具、スクリーンといった要素に色を振り分け、グラフィカルに空間を構成した。

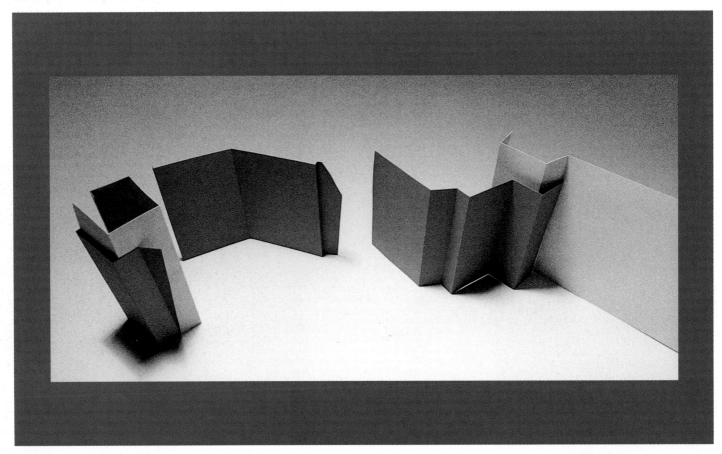

Tsubame City is famous as Japan's leading silverware production region. This silverware showroom was opened by the local wholesalers as an antenna shop in one of the city's downtown department stores.

The planning began with a decision on colors, with the choices being natural brown and blue.

The first color coincides with the color of the wooden tables where silverware is generally used. This color produces the feeling of an everyday space. Blue, on the other hand, was chosen as a non-everyday color which would be effective for the display of the silverware pieces. This color elevates the products to the forefront.

Each element of the interior design was considered from the standpoint of optimizing the effect of color. Steel panels, shelves, furnishings and screens were all given distinct colors, creating a graphically structured interior space.

1～3. ディスプレイテーブル	DISPLAY TABLE
4～5. 棚	SHELF
6. スクリーン	SCREEN
7. カウンター	COUNTER
8. 家具コーナー	FURNITURE DISPLAY CORNER
9. ストックルーム	STOCK ROOM

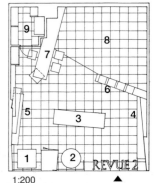

1:200

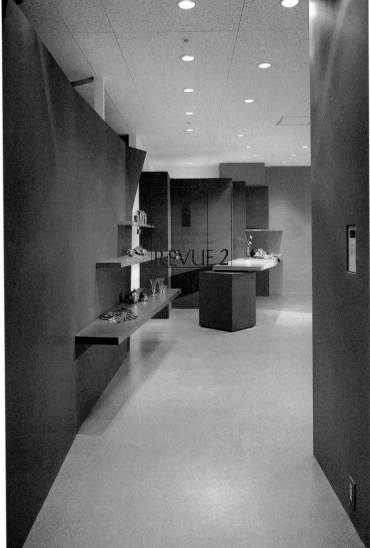

空間は作り込んだ仰々しい感じではなく、さりげない感じが出るよう、家具だけでなく、棚も、壁も、パネルも、自然に並べていったような構成になっている。特にスティールパネルには、折り紙のような形態を与え、視覚的に重さを取り除き、何気なくそこに置いてあるという感じを出している。

Rather than creating a sanctimonious effect, the interior aims to be a nonchalant setting, utilizing not only furniture but shelves, walls and panelling in a natural manner. The steel panels in particular were given a folded paper appearance, removing the sense of mass, suggesting that they were positioned indifferently.

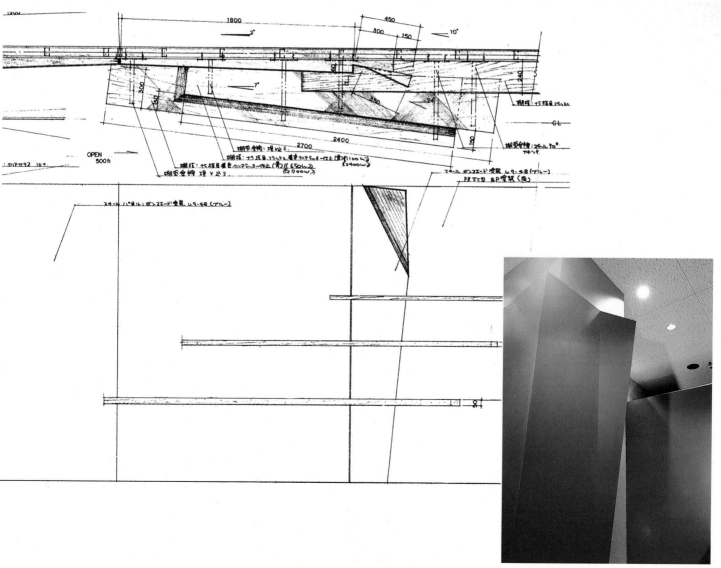

EDIC STUDIO
エディック・スタジオ
SENDAGAYA－TOKYO
東京－千駄ヶ谷

照明メーカーのオフィスに併設されたスタジオである。ここでは製品である照明器具の効果を見られるのは勿論、計画中のインテリアや建築の照明プランの具体的なプレゼンテーションができるようになっている。簡単な造作さえすれば、天井や壁に組み込まれたシステムで、コンピュータ、音響とともにディスコを体験させることも可能である。また、インテリアデザイナー、建築家はもとより、一般の人々にも照明をより身近なものに感じてもらうため、ここをギャラリーやイベントスペースとしても開放していこうとした。

多目的な用途に合わせ、スペースの脇に打合せのためのブースと、バー仕立てのサービスカウンター、入口にはスクリーンを兼ねたサンプルケースが設けてある。ここは本来の機能を果たしながら、同時に常設の具体的造作物として照明の実験が行えるようになっている。カウンターバックを除き、壁の仕上げはスペースと同じく白の塗装だけである。素材による表現はなく、主役の光を得て初めて表情が生まれる。光の向きにより影の形が変わり、立体は生き物のように変化する。鉄筋による線の密集からできる面、また線と線を面でつないでいくことによってできる彫刻的な立体。光と影を強調するべく、ドラマチックなデザインにしている。

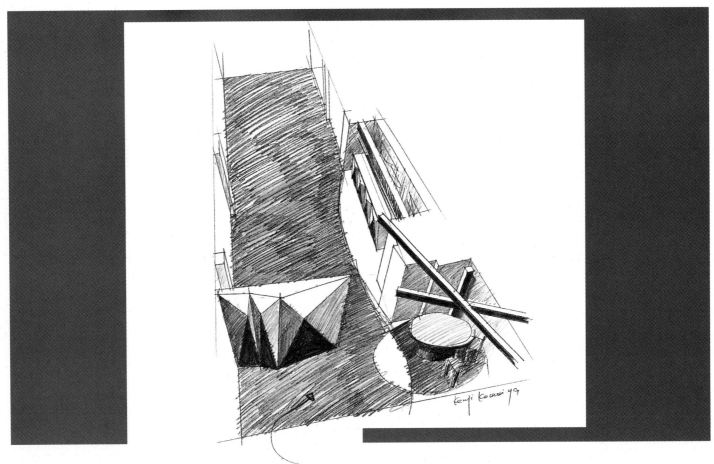

This space is a lighting manufacturer's combined studio. Naturally, the effects of various lighting fixtures can be observed here ; the space was designed specifically for the presentation of architectural lighting plans. With some simple manipulations of the ceiling and walls, and the use of a computer and sound system, one can even experience a discotique. This location is open to the public as an event space and gallery, so that not only interior designers and architects but people in general can experience firsthand the effects of lighting.

In order to satisfy the space's multi-purpose objectives, there is a booth and a service counter against one wall where meetings can be held, as well as a screen at the entrance which serves as a sample display case. This covers the needs of the office, while leaving a space where the every day work of product testing can be performed. With the exception of the counter, all the walls are painted the same white color as the rest of the space. Thus there is no material expression, only the first performance of the lighting itself. Changes in the direction of the light alter the shapes of shadows and bring life to solid bodies. These objects include surfaces made of densely packed steel rod, or surfaces connected by lines, which appear like sculpted shapes in the space. The interior is a dramatic design conceived to stress the interplay of light and shadow.

1. サンプル棚	SAMPLE DISPLAY SHELF	
2. 打合せ室	MEETING ROOM	
3. バーカウンター	BAR COUNTER	
4. スタジオ	STUDIO	
5. 操作室	OPERATION ROOM	
6. 化粧室	TOILET	

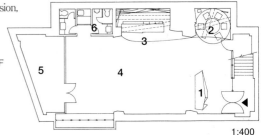

1:400

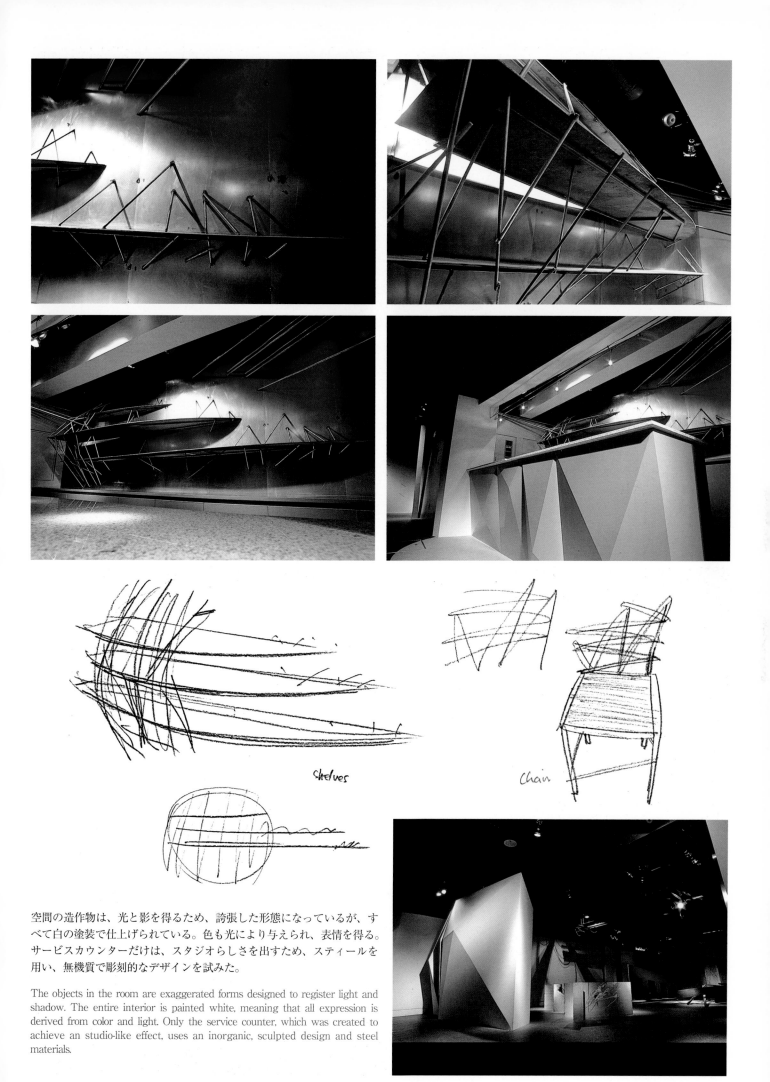

shelves

chair

空間の造作物は、光と影を得るため、誇張した形態になっているが、すべて白の塗装で仕上げられている。色も光により与えられ、表情を得る。サービスカウンターだけは、スタジオらしさを出すため、スティールを用い、無機質で彫刻的なデザインを試みた。

The objects in the room are exaggerated forms designed to register light and shadow. The entire interior is painted white, meaning that all expression is derived from color and light. Only the service counter, which was created to achieve an studio-like effect, uses an inorganic, sculpted design and steel materials.

About the S T E E L
スティールについて

素材の中でスティールは私の最も好きなものの一つである。それは、その素材感が特に好きというわけではなく、私のフォルムを自在に実現してくれるからである。
"曲げる""折る""線で接合する""点で接合する""薄くする""細くする"ということが、

この素材の特徴である強度、張力、溶接で可能になる。
スティールはあくまでフォルムの実現のための手段であり、仕上げに塗装が施されたり、天然木のつき板が張られたりして、最終的には布や木や紙のような他の表情を得ることに

なる。宙に舞った帯（クレヨン・インターセクション）や、折り紙（レビュー）、波打つ板（ノイバンシュタイン）、水中に揺らめく海草（ヘヴン）、カッターで切り込まれた紙（ワープ）等、数々のオブジェがスティールで製作されている。

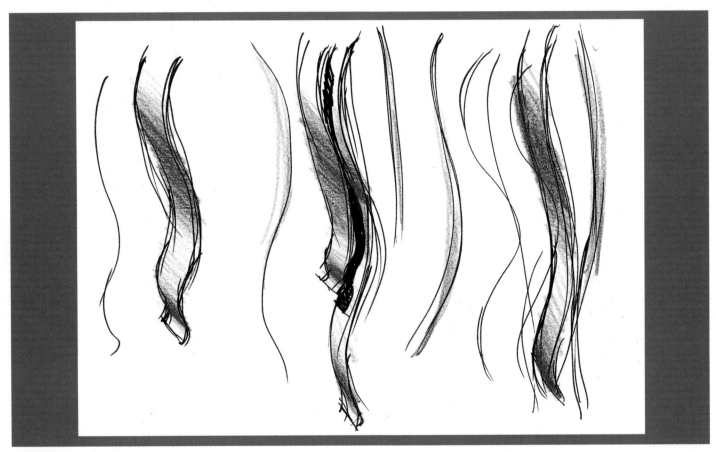

Of all materials I like steel the most. This is not so much because I like the feel of the material, but because steel frees me to create so many forms.

The special properties of steel—its bendability, its foldability, its ability to be connected by lines or points, its workability in thin or fine forms—are

made possible by its hardness, tensility and weldability.

I invariably use steel as a method to create shapes, and later paint it, add natural wood sheet, or some other material, trying to create a final expression more along the lines of cloth or wood

or paper. Many of the objects I have created, including belts that dance in space (Crayon Intersection), folded paper (Revue), waved paneling (Noivan Stein), seaweed waving underwater (Heaven) and paper cut into paper (Warp) are built with steel.

CRAYON INTERSECTION
クレヨン・インターセクション

着物と洋服の混合ブティックである。左側に着物、右側に洋服を配し、中央のディスプレイには対峙する2種の衣服が同じ台の上に乗っている。この領域分けをするべく、着物の帯をイメージしたオブジェが、空に舞う天女の羽衣のごとくふわふわと立ち昇っている。このオブジェには2mmのスティールに塗装が施されている。

This boutique presents both western and Japanese style apparel. The kimonos are on the left side, the western apparel on the right. In the middle are displays with both genres, separated by objects that look like kimono belts, or angels' robes, floating in the air. The objects are made of 2mm thick painted steel.

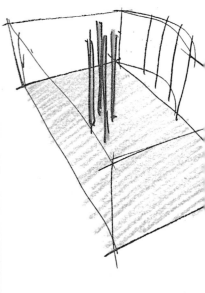

HEAVEN

ヘヴン

海の中をイメージしたイタリアン・レストランである。海中にゆらめく海草のオブジェがスティールで作られている。ここではその他、光の揺らぐ水面が天井部のアクリルの波板で、水の動きが壁に埋め込まれたガラスで光とともに表現されている。

This Italian restaurant takes the undersea for its motif. The seaweed objects are made of steel, while the surface of the sea sparkling in the sunlight is expressed by the waved acrylic of the ceiling, and the movement of the water is shown in the glass embedded in the walls.

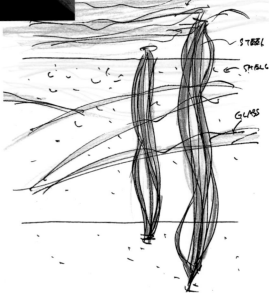

NISHI STYLES　ニシ・スタイルズ

林立する柱が空間に縦の軸を与え、また前後のコーナーを発生させる。エレガントなブティックを象徴するように、ステンレスの鏡面仕上げとなっている。

The poles in the center of the room give the space its axis, and enliven the corners behind and in front of it. The boutique's elegant ambience is brought out by the polished stainless steel.

EVE MUSEUM　イブ・ミュージアム

一陣の風が辺りを揺らしながら吹き込んできた。うなぎの寝床のような空間で、客の視線を奥まで導くために仕掛けられたオブジェである。

A rush of wind crashes about and then blows inside the place. In this narrow and long space the object is designed to lead the beholder's eye to the back of the shop.

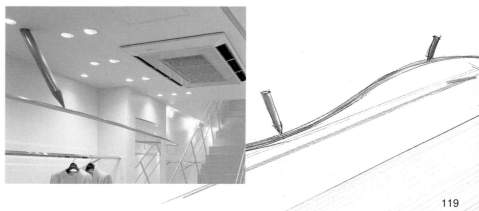

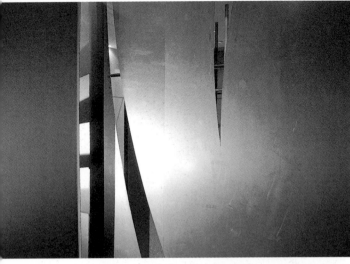

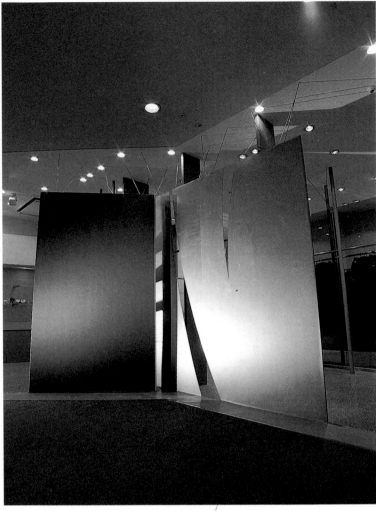

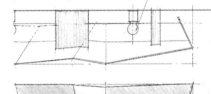

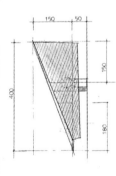

WARP ワープ

カッターで切り込んだ紙。緊張感
あふれるその一瞬の表現は、張力
のあるスティールならではである。

Paper cut with a cutter. The tension of
that instant can be captured with the
tensile strength of steel.

A−HOUSE A邸

ブラケットランプは無造作に開い
た感じを出している。人為的な形
態が居室に優しさを与えている。

A-House
The bracket lamps appear to have
been cut naturally into their places.
These forms of human-like creation
lend a softness to the interior.

UCC CAFÉ PLAZA

UCCカフェプラザ

"混乱"を表現するために壁面に張り巡らされたL型スティールは、オブジェであると同時に壁面のブラケットランプにもなっている。

The L-form steel wall object expresses "confusion" but also serves as the bracket lamp of the interior.

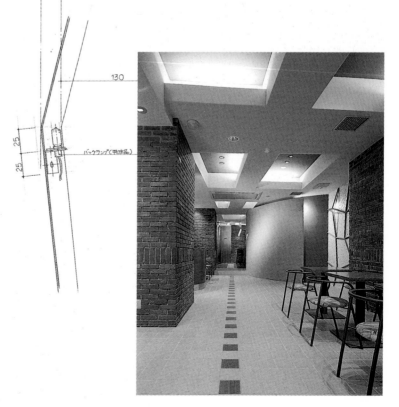

CHAIR, LAMP & TABLE WARE
椅子・照明器具・テーブルウェア

家具やランプ、テーブルウェアは空間において ポイントになるだけでなく、時として全体 の意味を決定してしまうこともある。従って ほとんどの場合、空間の一部とし、物件ごと にオリジナルのデザインを起こしている。 それとは別に、これらはそれだけで私の建築 や空間のコンセプトを表現するツールとなる ため、クライアントからの条件を伴わない純 粋なデザイン作業として、強いメッセージを 込めて製作している。

These objects are not only points in a space; at times, they are the objects which lend the entire space its meaning. For this reason in most cases these objects are created as original elements of the design. However, I often design these objects to express a concept of architecture or space, as well as pure design, irrespective of the client's wishes, intending to convey a strong message.

122頁
FOAK, KNIFE, SPOON "FLYING"
フォーク、ナイフ、スプーン "飛行"
（ステンレス製）
空気の流れを表現したステンレス筋はスプリングになっており、しっかりしたグリップ効果が得られる。

(Stainless)
Expressing the flow of air, this stainless steel acts as a spring, offering an excellent grip.

123頁　上
LAMP "CLOUD"
ランプ "雲"
波型プラスチック板を使ったスタンドランプと卓上ランプである。この他、ペンダントとブラケットもある。白く軽い雲のようなランプである。

p.123 top
This lampstand and table lamp were created with waved plastic sheet. There are also pendant and bracket style lamps. These lamps are white in color and light like clouds.

123頁　下
LAMP "PICCOLA ARCHITETTURA"
ランプ "ピッコラ・アルキテットゥーラ"
光を放つ都市をミニチュア化したランプである。ビー玉を替えることにより、光の色が変えられる。着脱可能な建築の提案である。

p. 123 lower
A lamp suggesting the light given off by a miniature city. By changing the glass balls the color of the light can be changed. This is a proposal for wear and remove architecture.

左上
LAMP "WING"
ランプ "翼"
ステンレス製のパンチングメタルと波型アクリルを合わせた傘は、水平の回転と上下動をする。

Upper left
This shade of punched stainless steel and acrylic creates a turning, undulating horizon.

左中
TABLE "K"
テーブル "K"
ミニマムなトラス構造の脚をもつテーブルである。

Middle left
A table with minimal leg structural supports.

左下
STAINLESS STEEL CHAIR "α"
ステンレス製チェア "α"
ステンレスベルトの座は座ると沈み込みがあり、クールな外見だが、意外にもソフトな座り心地である。

Lower left
This chair of stainless steel belts is not only cool to the eye but surprisingly comfortable, offering a cushiony feel.

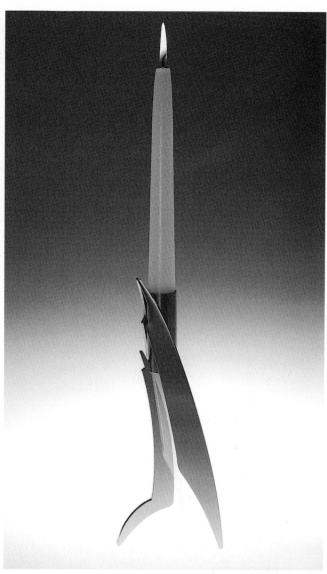

Upper

上: A VASE FOR JUST ONE STEM "WARP"
一輪ざし "ワープ"

Upper right
右上: CANDLE STAND "ROCKET"
キャンドルスタンド "ロケット"

Lower right
右下: FLOWER VASE "SPACE SHIP"
花びん "スペースシップ"

DATA

小森谷賢二　Kenji Komoriya

1955年、群馬県生まれ。明治大学工学部建築学科卒業。ハナエ・モリ・グループにインテリア・デザイナーとして勤務の後、1984年独立、株式会社ヴィンチを設立。インテリアデザインを中心に建築及び商業施設の計画・設計、ストリートファニチャー、家具・照明器具等のデザインも手がけている。
他方、イタリアの都市と建築に魅せられ、写真を撮り続けている。
明治大学理工学部建築学科 非常勤講師。
宮城大学事業構想学部デザイン情報学科
非常勤講師。

著書　魅惑のローマ（グラフィック社・共著）
　　　シチリアへ行きたい（新潮社・共著）
　　　ローマ古代散歩（新潮社・共著）

連絡先：東京都渋谷区神宮前2-35-13
　　　　原宿リビン505
　　　　TEL 03-3404-3777
　　　　FAX 03-3497-1447
　　　　#505, Harajuku Livin, 2-35-13
　　　　Jingumae, Shibuya-ku, Tokyo
　　　　JAPAN

ヴィンチスタッフ
　　　関　徹郎＊
　　　村山　清＊
　　　金野　克己＊
　　　道下　泰
　　　（＊印　元所員）

INTERIOR DESIGN
インテリア・デザイン 発想と設計

1998年10月25日　初版第1刷発行

著者　　　小森谷賢二
発行者　　久世利郎
印刷・製本　日本写真印刷株式会社
DTP作成　デザインルーム air
発行所　　株式会社グラフィック社
　　　　　〒102-0073　東京都千代田区九段下1-9-12
　　　　　電話 03-3263-4318　FAX 03-3263-5297